Contemporary Newsmakers

ISSN 0883-1564

Contemporary Newsmakers

A Biographical Guide to People in the News in Business, Education, Technology, Social Issues, Politics, Law, Economics, International Affairs, Religion, Entertainment, Labor, Sports, Design, Psychology, Medicine, Astronautics, Ecology, and Other Fields

Ann Evory and Peter M. Gareffa
Editors

1985
Issue 2

Indexes to
1985, Issues 1-2

GALE RESEARCH COMPANY • BOOK TOWER • DETROIT, MICHIGAN 48226

STAFF

Ann Evory and Peter M. Gareffa, *Editors*

Denise Wiloch, *Assistant Editor*

Joseph A. Kuskowski, *Editorial Assistant*

Amy C. Bodwin and Gary Hoffman, *Interviewers*

Mary Rose Bonk, Christine Joan May, and Mary Alice Rattenbury, *Research Assistants*

Amy C. Bodwin, Ingeborg Boyens, Victoria France Charabati, Lori R. Clemens, Gary Graff, John E. Haynes,
Gary Hoffman, Tom Hundley, Tim Kiska, Michael L. LaBlanc, Joe LaPointe, James G. Lesniak, Anita Lienert,
Paul Lienert, Glen Macnow, Patricia Montemurri, Barbara Welch Skaggs, Mary Solomon Smyka,
Susan Stefani, Susan M. Trosky, and Thomas Wiloch, *Contributing Editors*

Jeanne Gough, *Permissions Supervisor*
Patricia A. Seefelt, *Permissions Coordinator, Illustrations*
Margaret A. Chamberlain, *Senior Permissions Assistant*

Carol Blanchard, *Production Director*
Dorothy Kalleberg, *Production Associate*
Arthur Chartow, *Art Director*

Frederick G. Ruffner, *Publisher*
James M. Ethridge, *Executive Vice-President/Editorial*
Dedria Bryfonski, *Editorial Director*
Christine Nasso, *Director, Literature Division*

Copyright © 1985 by Gale Research Company

ISBN 0-8103-2200-5
ISSN 0883-1564

Computerized photocomposition by
AMTEC, Inc.
Lakewood, California

Contents

Preface 7

Newsmakers Forthcoming in *CN* 11

Cumulative Newsmaker Index 111

Cumulative Nationality Index 113

Cumulative Occupation Index 115

Cumulative Subject Index 117

Preface

"There is properly no history, only biography."
—Ralph Waldo Emerson, *History*

Since history is written through the actions of men and women, biography is an important tool to help us understand our present and our past. Unfortunately, comprehensive biographical information on people currently in the news is often difficult to find. With the publication of *Contemporary Newsmakers (CN)*, Gale Research Company has taken a step toward remedying that situation.

Since 1962, Gale has published *Contemporary Authors (CA)*, a comprehensive source of information on current writers that is notably easy to use because of its unique format. Librarians have often pointed out to Gale editors the need for a series that covers reference-worthy "nonwriters" in the same depth as *CA* covers major writers. *CN* is designed to do this.

For those people currently in the news, *CN* provides personal and career data in an easy-to-use format that presents facts in captioned paragraphs. Narrative accounts of subjects' views and achievements are presented in informative sidelights written in a clear, readable style, quoting evaluations and comments from the listees' peers, friends, and critics. Most entries contain portraits of the newsmakers, and some include additional photographs specially selected to complement sidelights material. Finally, for some subjects an exclusive interview is provided.

From students writing papers on topical issues to general readers interested in current events and the people behind them, *CN* is designed to assist a variety of users. Teachers preparing assignments, researchers seeking facts, and librarians fielding questions can all turn to *CN* for detailed entries on the people making today's news. Just as *CA* meets the need for information on writers, *CN* serves an equally broad range of users who need information on nonwriters. Normally, no overlap between *CA* and *CN* will occur.

Scope and Frequency

CN is a comprehensive biographical guide to people in the news in such fields as business, education, technology, social issues, politics, law, economics, international affairs, religion, entertainment, labor, sports, design, psychology, medicine, astronautics, and ecology. *CN* provides biographical material on newsmakers in two broad categories—individuals who are quite well known and about whom information is widely available in newspapers and magazines but not in reference books, and people who are less well known but who, because of the importance or interesting nature of their activities, are currently in the news and are deserving of wider coverage.

The emphasis of *CN* is on those people involved in topical issues; for example, an entry on Nabih Berri, the Lebanese Shiite Muslim leader who acted as a negotiator during the 1985 TWA hostage crisis, is included in this issue, as is a profile of Nanette Falkenberg, head of the National Abortion Rights Action League.

CN is published quarterly in a paperbound format. Each *CN* issue, identified by a year and issue number, is about 100 pages long and covers approximately fifty newsmakers. All entries in each year's quarterly issues will also be available in an annual clothbound cumulation.

CN Differs from Existing Biographical Sources

The editors believe *CN* satisfies a need unmet by existing reference tools. Although *Current Biography* does an admirable job of providing biographical information on some important people of the day, there are far more newsworthy individuals than can be covered by a single source. *CN* will profile approximately 200 newsmakers per year. It is the intention of the editors not to include in *CN* full sketches on those people who have up-to-date entries in *Current Biography*.

Other biographical sources, such as Newsbank's *Names in the News,* cover an impressive number of people but contain only reprinted material that does not necessarily highlight or include important career and personal data. Indexes such as *Biography Index* and Gale's own *Biography Almanac* are valuable reference tools but serve a different function than a biographical source such as *CN.* The *Who's Who* publications provide important information, but it is not in their scope to supply the kind of sidelights that many students and researchers need. In addition to presenting rich sidelights material, *CN* differs from the *Who's Who* publications in its greater frequency and in its scope, which concentrates on the innovators who help shape our culture and society—such as controversial pop singer Madonna—rather than established or establishment figures. In short, *CN* fills a gap on reference shelves.

Compilation Methods

As is the case with *CA,* the information contained within *CN* is secured directly from the subjects whenever possible. Through questionnaires, personal correspondence, and telephone calls, the editors make every effort to contact the biographees slated for an upcoming issue. For example, contributing editor Gary Hoffman, during the course of his telephone interview with feminist attorney Gloria Allred, was able to secure from Allred some of the personal information included in her *CN* sketch.

If persons of special interest to *CN* users fail to reply to requests for information, the editors gather data from other reliable sources, including published interviews, feature stories, news articles, etc., and verify this information later with the subjects if possible.

The editors recognize that entries on particularly active newsmakers may eventually become outdated. To insure *CN*'s timeliness, future issues will provide revisions of selected sketches when they require significant change.

Format

The format of *CN* is similar to that of *CA,* with one important addition—*CN* includes portraits of the subjects, when available. In selected entries, additional illustrations of people and events important to the listees' careers also enliven the text.

So that a reader needing specific information can quickly focus on the pertinent portion of an entry, typical *CN* sketches are clearly divided into the following sections:

Entry heading—Cites the form of the name by which the listee is best known, as well as birth and death dates, when available.

Personal—Provides the newsmaker's full name if different from the entry heading, date and place of birth, family data, and information about the subject's education, politics, and religion.

Addresses—Notes home and office addresses, when available.

Occupation—Identifies the listee's primary fields of activity.

Career—Indicates past and present career positions, with inclusive dates, as well as civic activities and military service.

Member—Highlights memberships in various professional and civic associations and official posts held.

Awards, honors—Lists awards and honors received.

Sidelights—Provides a personal dimension to the entry and fills in the details that make for interesting biography. Subjects are encouraged to supply comments on their work and interests. Whether these remarks are long or short, serious or humorous, they are incorporated into sidelights with minimal editing, in the belief that they make possible a better understanding of the biographee.

In addition to the subjects' own comments, sidelights explain why these people are in the news and detail their rise to prominence. For instance, in this issue, contributing editor Amy

C. Bodwin traces Brandon Tartikoff's career from his first job in the promotion department of the ABC affiliate station in New Haven, Connecticut, through his successes in television programming in Chicago and New York, to his present position as president of NBC Entertainment in Burbank, California.

Sources—Lists magazine and newspaper articles and books containing additional information on the biographees.

When applicable, *CN* sketches include "Discography" sections that provide information on songs or albums recorded by the biographees. To provide a complete record of newsmakers' accomplishments, a few *CN* sketches necessarily contain "Writings" sections that list books and articles, often of a specialized nature, written by the listees. Potential *CN* subjects known primarily as writers, however, fall outside the scope of *CN;* their entries would appear instead in *CA*.

Exclusive Interviews

In addition to the information noted above, selected *CN* sketches also contain exclusive interviews with the newsmakers. Prepared specifically for *CN,* the never-before-published conversations presented in the section of the entry headed *"CN* Interview" give readers an opportunity to learn the subjects' thoughts, in depth, about their careers and interests. This issue features interviews with feminist attorney Gloria Allred and anti-nuclear power activist Mary Sinclair.

Brief Entries and Obituary Notices Make *CN* Timely and Comprehensive

The editors feel that having some information, however brief, on individuals very recently in the news is preferable to waiting until full-length sketches can be prepared. Some abbreviated listings for such persons are included in *CN*. These short profiles, identified by the heading "Brief Entry," highlight the subjects' careers, provide sources where additional information can be found, and include portraits, when available.

Brief entries are not intended to replace sketches. Instead, brief entries maintain *CN's* currency and comprehensiveness by covering people just coming into the news—as exemplified by the brief entry in this issue on Trevor Ferrell, the young Philadelphia man who initiated a campaign to aid street people—and providing basic data about newsworthy individuals on whom little information is currently available—such as Robert Anastas, founder of Students Against Drunken Driving (SADD). All newsmakers receiving brief entry coverage may be the subjects of full sketches in forthcoming issues.

CN also publishes obituary notices on deceased newsmakers within the scope of the series. These notices provide dates and places of birth and death, highlight the subjects' careers, and list other sources where information can be found. Photographs are also included, when available. The heading "Obituary Notice" distinguishes obituaries from full-length sketches.

Obituary coverage will not be limited to people with previous *CN* entries but will include a wide variety of recently deceased newsmakers. As a result of our efforts to provide obituary information on key figures in the news, *CN* may occasionally duplicate obituaries in other biographical sources.

Indexes

To best serve the needs of a wide variety of users by providing access to entries in a number of ways, *CN* contains cumulative newsmaker, nationality, occupation, and subject indexes. Each of these indexes will continue to be cumulated in future quarterly issues and the annual hardcover cumulations.

Cumulative Newsmaker Index—Biographee names, along with birth and death dates, when available, are arranged alphabetically followed by the *CN* year and issue number in which their entries appear. References to obituary notices and brief entries contained in *CN* are clearly designated as such. Cross-references from the subjects' full names to the more common forms of their names used in the entry headings are also included in the Cumulative Newsmaker Index.

Cumulative Nationality Index—Listee names are arranged alphabetically under their respective nationalities and are followed by the *CN* year and issue number in which the entries are included. The Cumulative Nationality Index reflects the diversity of newsmakers covered in *CN;* this issue, for example, contains listings on Canadian, Japanese, Lebanese, and Soviet figures, among others, who have recently been in the news.

Cumulative Occupation Index—All newsmakers' names, with references to the *CN* year and issue number containing their entries, are listed alphabetically under broad occupational categories or fields of primary activity. Readers interested in surveying recent developments in business, for example, will find entries on MCI Communications chairman William McGowan, Edmonton Oilers owner Peter H. Pocklington, and Toyota Motor Corp. chairman Eiji Toyoda, among others, in this issue.

Cumulative Subject Index—This index includes citations to key subjects, topical issues, company names, products, organizations, awards, etc., that are discussed in *CN.* Under each subject citation are listed newsmakers associated with that topic and the year and issue number in which their entries appear.

The Cumulative Subject Index is designed to allow access to the facts in *CN,* even when readers are unfamiliar with the names of individuals associated with a particular topic. A student interested in writing a paper on drunk driving, for example, will be directed to information on this topic through the citations for "Drunk driving" and "Alcohol abuse" in the Cumulative Subject Index, which will refer the student to the full-length sketch in *CN* 1985, Issue 1, on Candy Lightner, founder of Mothers Against Drunk Driving (MADD), and the brief entry in 1985, Issue 2, on Robert Anastas, founder of Students Against Drunken Driving (SADD).

Including citations ranging from "Atari" to "Women's rights," the Cumulative Subject Index not only leads to answers to specific questions but also invites browsing, allowing *CN* users to discover topics they may wish to explore further.

Suggestions Are Welcome

The editors welcome comments and suggestions from users to enhance the usefulness of this series. If readers would like to suggest newsmakers to be covered in future *CN* issues, they are encouraged to send these names to the editors.

Newsmakers Forthcoming in *CN*

Listed Below Are a Few of the Individuals Being Considered for Future *CN* 1985 Issues

Kathy Baker
Professional golfer; winner of 1985 U.S. Women's Open

Boris Becker
West German tennis player; winner of men's singles at Wimbledon, 1985

Billy Crystal
Comedian and actor

Ray Dolby
Electrical engineer; president of Dolby Labs, Inc., and inventor of Dolby noise reduction system

Robert M. Fomon
Chairman of E.F. Hutton & Co. brokerage firm

David Geffen
Record, film, and theatrical producer

Bob Geldof
Lead singer with Boomtown Rats; initiated Band Aid and Live Aid projects for African famine relief

Donald Graham
Newspaper executive; head of Washington Post Co.

Bob Guccione
Magazine executive; founder and publisher of Penthouse and Omni

Mark Hughes
Entrepreneur; founder and president of Herbalife International

Arthur Jones
Entrepreneur; inventor of Nautilus exercise machines and head of Nautilus Sports/Medical Industries

Bobby Knight
Controversial basketball coach at Indiana University

Jari Kurri
Professional hockey player for Edmonton Oilers

Robin Leach
Host of television's "Lifestyles of the Rich and Famous"

Dan Marino
Quarterback for Miami Dolphins; led team to the 1985 Super Bowl

Vince McMahon
Head of World Wrestling Federation; credited with resurgence in popularity of professional wrestling

Christian Petrossian
French importer; leading supplier of Russian caviar to the United States

John J. Phelan, Jr.
President of New York Stock Exchange and chairman of New York Futures Exchange

Christopher Pratt
Canadian surrealist artist

Patrick Redig
Veterinarian; specialist in treating birds of prey

Molly Ringwald
Actress; appeared in "Tempest," "Sixteen Candles," "The Breakfast Club"

Xavier Roberts
Folk artist; founder and chairman of Original Appalachian Artworks, Inc., and creator of Cabbage Patch dolls

D. Douglas Roth
Lutheran minister jailed for protest activities against U.S. Steel and Mellon Bank in Pennsylvania

Sade
Nigerian-born British singer

Marge Schott
Flamboyant owner of Cincinnati Reds and president of Schottco Corp.

John Josef Sedelmaier
Award-winning director of television commercials for Wendy's and Federal Express

Danny Sullivan
Professional race-car driver; winner of 1985 Indianapolis 500

Zehdi Labib Terzi
Palestinian representative to the United Nations

Kathleen Turner
Actress; appeared in "Body Heat," "Romancing the Stone," "Prizzi's Honor"

Faye Wattleton
President of Planned Parenthood Federation of America

Gloria Allred

1941-

PERSONAL: Full name, Gloria Rachel Allred; born July 3, 1941, in Philadelphia, Pa.; daughter of Morris Bloom and Stella Davidson; married, 1960 (divorced); married Raymond Allred (an aircraft parts dealer), 1968; children: Lisa (first marriage). *Education*: University of Pennsylvania, B.A. (with honors in English), 1963; New York University, M.A., 1966; Loyola University, J.D. (with honors), 1974.

ADDRESSES: Office—6380 Wilshire Blvd., Suite 1404, Los Angeles, Calif. 90048.

OCCUPATION: Attorney.

CAREER: High-school English teacher in Philadelphia, Pa., for two years, and Los Angeles, Calif., for four years; labor organizer for Los Angeles Teachers' Association for one year; Allred, Maroko, Goldberg & Ribakoff (law firm), Los Angeles, founder and partner, 1975—. Lecturer, University of Southern California, 1976—. Advance person for Brown for Governor Campaign, 1974; bureau coordinator for Carter Campaign, 1976.

MEMBER: National Organization for Women (coordinator, Los Angeles chapter, 1977—), Save Equal Rights Amendment (chairperson), Delta Theta Phi.

AWARDS, HONORS: Outstanding Citizen Award, Southgate Business and Professional Women's Club, 1976; certificate of appreciation, American Women in Radio and Television.

WRITINGS: Contributor of articles to periodicals.

SIDELIGHTS: To her opponents, Gloria Allred is a feisty, feminist lawyer, more interested in furthering pet causes than in practicing law. To her admirers, she is a rebel in the tradition of the civil rights activists of the 1960s or the muckrakers of the Teddy Roosevelt era. Her controversial cases have made her a force to be reckoned with in California politics, and her influence has spread across the United States. She has represented a homosexual seeking the right to adopt a child, has sought child custody rights for the father of an illegitimate child, and has made headlines by prompting groundbreaking family-rights legislation.

CN INTERVIEW

CN interviewed Gloria Allred by telephone at her office in Los Angeles, Calif., in June, 1985.

CN: What category fits you best? Is feminist a fair description?

ALLRED: Sure, I'm a feminist. I'm a feminist attorney. How's that?

AP/Wide World Photos

CN: How does this square with your representing LeVar Burton in his lawsuit to gain joint custody of his illegitimate child?

ALLRED: How about, "consistently"? Absolutely consistently.

CN: How's that?

ALLRED: Well, he was a father who wished to play a major role in his son's life even though he had not been married to the mother of the child and wasn't going to be married to the mother of the child. He still felt that he would like to have joint legal custody of the child and take an active role in his life. And I think it's important that he and other single fathers play that role, because children need the love and support of both parents. So I was very happy to support him in that, and I am always encouraging fathers to take an active role. But it turns out that a lot of fathers who've never been married to the mothers decide not to take any part in the child's life.

CN: And so you were removing a potential legal obstacle to his having a normal relationship with his child?

13

ALLRED: Well, I succeeded in supporting his wishes that he be able to take an active role in the child's life. And he did get joint custody of the child and the visitation rights that he wanted. He was a role model for other fathers, to encourage them to become active in their children's lives.

CN: How do you describe the cases that you and your firm specialize in?

ALLRED: Well, we're a civil litigation firm, we have thirteen attorneys, and we do all kinds of civil litigation. I suppose we're best known for family law cases and for civil rights cases.

CN: But you don't do that exclusively?

ALLRED: No, we also do business litigation and personal injuries, as well as family law and civil rights.

CN: So, your practice is probably far more general than has often been described?

ALLRED: Absolutely. In fact, we're the cover story on the *American Bar Association Journal* this month. It looks at the practice and how we handle different cases. Most people don't know that we are very diversified as civil litigators.

CN: Is the activist role, in both your personal ideology and your law practice, filling a void among law firms? Are you filling a need that isn't satisfied elsewhere?

ALLRED: In terms of what?

CN: Would you expect that the representation, say, of a woman raped in a shopping mall is better handled by a firm like yours than the typical firm? Or one where the majority of people are male?

ALLRED: Well, I feel that men are not the enemy, and women are not the enemy, ignorance is the enemy. And I always think it's better for anyone to be represented by a feminist than to be represented by a non-feminist.

CN: On any sort of case?

ALLRED: Whether it's a feminist male or a feminist female. I consider the difference to be between feminist and non-feminist, rather than male and female, because men can be feminists. In fact, a requirement of working in this firm is that any attorney here must be a feminist.

CN: Now how do you. . . ?

ALLRED: I ask them.

CN: You ask them?

ALLRED: We discuss it. Yeah.

CN: What if you meet someone who doesn't describe himself as a feminist but is an altogether honorable and fair person? What if he just doesn't happen to use that term to describe himself?

ALLRED: Well, we discuss what the term means. The dictionary defines it as a person who believes in legal, social, political, and economic equality for women with men. So I think it is very important for me to have people who believe in legal, political, social, and economic equality for women with men working here in the law firm. And anyone who doesn't believe in that kind of equality is either a male chauvinist or a racist, or both. That type of person, will need to look for work elsewhere, because they're not going to be here.

CN: What percent of your cases are civil rights cases?

ALLRED: Well, those, I guess, are the ones we're the most visible on, but actually they are a small percent of the actual law practice. We do a lot of day-to-day divorce cases. They are not issues of public interest or importance to other people and so, therefore, are not on the news. In fact, they are confidential, and should be confidential between the parties. But these cases that we do that are civil rights court cases *are* of public interest and importance and do have an impact on many people. And they are the ones most in the news, even though they are a smaller percent of our cases, in fact, than family law cases, for example.

CN: Was the LeVar Burton representation atypical? Do you represent a lot of celebrities?

ALLRED: I wouldn't say a lot of celebrities. We've represented some celebrities. We've represented, for example, Lynn Redgrave, the actress, in her case against Universal. We were suing them because we alleged that she was terminated from the hit series "House Calls" because she wanted to breast-feed her baby during a break in the filming. So that's a sex-discrimination civil-rights type of case. I've represented McKenzie Phillips, another actress ("One Day at a Time"), on a spousal support issue she had with her ex-husband. He was seeking alimony from her. So we have represented some celebrities and still do, but I would say that a large part of our practice is the typical person who has been wronged or is in need of protection and representation. Vigorous representation. Assertive representation. We handle a lot of those cases, and we do also have a lot of precedent-setting cases and cases that will be called "cases of first impression," unusual cases making new law. Probably much more of those cases than most law firms ever have.

CN: And that's because you're on the cutting edge of some social issues?

ALLRED: I guess. Well, a lot of people, when they have unusual issues, interesting issues, important issues, they come to us. A lot of times they have gone to other attorneys, and the other attorneys don't even *see* the issue. Or they see it, and they don't want to get involved with it. Then we listen to it, and if we think it's important—and if we have the resources at that time, if we can 'make the time commitment and so forth—we tend to assist these.

CN: Has the much publicized increasing conservative inclination of the country had an effect on doing battle on legal grounds? Has it made it more important for people to have access to the courts?

ALLRED: I think it's always important for people to have access to the courts. Particularily women, and minorities, too, in the past have not had access. Now we have, in the last twenty years begun to have new rights, and we need to educate people about those rights and help them to vindicate those rights by providing access to the courts. Otherwise it is meaningless to have rights.

CN: Would the actual seeking the exercising of these rights in court be more important as society becomes, perhaps, more conservative?

ALLRED: I think it is always important. But yes, I do think so. I do think that change is accomplished when those who would prevent the change know that we are serious about having our rights. One of the ways they know we're serious about it is when we go to court to protect ourselves. And that's what we do when the matter cannot be resolved in an alternative way.

CN: You had a much publicized—I guess a feud might be the way to characterize it—with John Schmitz, a California state senator.

ALLRED: Yeah. It's still in litigation. We're waiting for a trial date. It's what you call "at issue."

CN: At one point you presented him with a chastity belt?

ALLRED: I presented it to him. It was at a hearing he was holding in Los Angeles when he was a state senator. He was proposing an amendment to our state constitution which would have eliminated the right to choose abortion and which would have eliminated many modern forms of birth control. And I presented the chastity belt to him after I testified.

CN: Did you get any criticisms from the legal community for this action?

ALLRED: Well, not particularily.

CN: It seems a bit flamboyant.

ALLRED: Yes. Well, you know I'm an activist.

CN: Are you an activist more than a lawyer?

ALLRED: No. I'm an activist lawyer. I believe in seeking change and winning rights through the legal process and also through the political process. And both of those go hand in hand. Sometimes the legal remedies are inadequate, and, therefore, we must utilize the political process by influencing public opinion, working to support new laws, and helping to educate our legislators about what we want to protect our rights. All of those things were involved in my presentation of the chastity belt. I wanted to draw the attention of the public to the fact that he was trying to eliminate the right to choose abortion and modern forms of birth control. And we didn't want him to go through all this without the public even knowing what was happening. A lot of times these hearings don't get covered, don't get noticed, and people lose their rights before they even know what happened to them.

CN: To what do you attribute the development of your particular brand of activism?

ALLRED: I would say I attribute it to life experience as a woman growing up in the United States of America. To give you more specifics, for example: being married as a teenager, giving birth to a child, getting divorced, not receiving child

support, basically having to raise a child by myself, getting paid less than a man in my first job for what I consider to be equal work and equal experience, having been raped, having to have an abortion when abortion was illegal and unsafe, almost dying from it. These are just a few of the things.

CN: Were you in favor of the availability of abortion even before your rape?

ALLRED: I have always been pro-choice.

CN: Even back when it was illegal?

ALLRED: Well, it wasn't illegal to *have* an abortion, it was illegal for a doctor to give it, which is an important distinction. I wasn't breaking any law. The law said that doctors couldn't perform abortions, and, therefore, young women like myself had to resort to being into the hands of butchers and quacks and almost dying; and some did, in fact, die. So, I have always been in favor of safe and legal abortions and the right to choose that, in support of women's rights. And certainly almost dying from an unsafe one, an illegal one, awoke me to the need to have safe and legal abortions and caused me to commit myself to forever fight for the right to have safe and legal abortions. I certainly would never want my daughter to be in the position that I was in and be in danger of dying from an illegal and unsafe abortion if it were necessary for her to have one.

CN: Do you get hate mail for your stands?

ALLRED: I get lots of thanks, and appreciation, and praise; and I also get some hate mail; I get some threats. I'm a lightning rod for change. A lot of people love me. Some people hate me. Generally, there's not too much in the way of middle ground. People come up to me in elevators, and parking lots, and street corners, and in court houses, in department stores, in restaurants and ask me for legal advice and help in solving their problems. And I am very happy that people feel that they have access to me and would like to have advice as to how to protect themselves. I would say, generally, most of it is positive because I am involved in very current issues, and by the definition of what I do, seeking rights for women is controversial, and, of course, there are going to be a lot of people who disagree with me—bigots— and those people will certainly express themselves most vociferously, as they always do.

CN: A caption in a Time *magazine article about you said, "Her tactics include turkeys, frogs, and chastity belts." How representative are those tactics of your work?*

ALLRED: Well, I'd say most of my battles are won in court. But sometimes a battle has to be waged in a different way. And so I do whatever I need to do in order to win the battle, as long as it's legal, and peaceful, and helps to win change. Sometimes that will include giving a chastity belt to a congressperson, or—one time—hanging diapers in the governor's office.

CN: You did that?

ALLRED: Yes. It was Jerry Brown, Jr., because he was set to veto a child-support bill that we had worked very hard to win; it was for a payroll deduction for child support to be taken out of the father's wages if he didn't pay. And his staff had written a letter saying that Brown was going to veto it.

So we ran down with mothers and children, and we hung diapers in there and held a press conference. And he tore up his veto message and signed the bill. So I'm saying, if it helps, I will do it. And in some cases it has helped, but I would say that ordinarily, ninety-nine percent of what I do, I do in a very traditional, conventional, yet assertive way. But sometimes it is necessary to be dramatic to make a point. We live in a media age and sometimes it is necessary to do that and I will continue to do that where it is helpful.

SOURCES:

PERIODICALS

Los Angeles, August, 1982.
Los Angeles Times, December 29, 1983, July 9, 1984, July 22, 1984, August 31, 1984.
Money, March, 1981.
New York Times, October 1, 1981, January 10, 1983.
Time, December 3, 1984.

—Interview by Gary Hoffman

Robert Anastas

BRIEF ENTRY: American teacher, counselor, social activist. Robert Anastas is the founder of Students Against Drunken Driving (SADD), a nationwide organization dedicated to informing teenagers of the dangers of drinking and driving. SADD employs a number of methods to get across its message, but the heart of the group's strategy is its "Drinking-Driver Contract." In this agreement, signed by both parents and teenagers, students promise to call their parents "for advice or transportation" in the event that "I have been drinking or a friend or date who is driving me has been drinking." In return, parents pledge to provide transportation "with no questions asked and no argument at that time." Parents also agree to "seek safe, sober transportation home" if they or whomever is driving "has had too much to drink."

Anastas, a high school teacher and substance abuse counselor, founded SADD in 1981 at Massachusetts's Wayland High School after two of his students died in alcohol-related accidents. Currently, there are SADD chapters in over 7,000 high schools throughout the country. The group has also launched programs aimed at college and elementary-school students. At all levels, SADD holds seminars and presents lectures and films that warn of the risks of driving while intoxicated. These measures notwithstanding, Anastas stresses the importance of the lifetime contract between parent and child. "All parents ought to sign the agreement—because they can't lecture their kids about booze or drugs after a fatal crash," he told Michael J. Weiss of the *Ladies Home Journal.* "Either pick them up now or get the hearse later." Address: SADD, Box 800, Marlboro, Mass. 01752.

Courtesy of SADD

SOURCES:

PERIODICALS

Glamour, February, 1985.
Ladies Home Journal, February, 1985.

Rosanna Arquette

1959-

PERSONAL: Born 1959, in New York; daughter of Lewis (a writer and director) and Mardi (a poet and playwright) Arquette.

ADDRESSES: Office—c/o Orion Pictures Co., 4000 Warner Blvd., Burbank, Calif. 91505.

OCCUPATION: Actress.

CAREER: Actress in television films, beginning 1978, including "Having Babies II," "Dark Secret of Harvest Home," "Zuma Beach," and "The Executioner's Song," and in motion pictures, beginning 1981, including "S.O.B.," "Baby It's You," "Desperately Seeking Susan," "After Hours," "Silverado," and "The Aviator."

SIDELIGHTS: In less than a decade Rosanna Arquette has gone from playing bit parts in forgettable made-for-television movies to star in such critically acclaimed feature films as *Desperately Seeking Susan.* Hailed as one of the freshest new faces in Hollywood, Arquette's stardom is unusual because her exposure as an actress has not been in commercial blockbusters but in low-budget art films. Arquette explained to *Moviegoer* interviewer Dale Pollock that she avoids doing roles simply for the sake of her career. Rather, she told him, "I do a movie for the character—what I'm going to put into the character or what I'm going to get out of the character. *That's* why I do a film."

Arquette was born into a theatrical family in New York in 1959. Her grandfather was Cliff Arquette who played Charley Weaver on *The Jack Parr Show* and *Hollywood Squares.* Arquette's father, Lewis, a writer and director, was formerly head of Chicago's improvisational comedy troupe, The Committee. In fact, Arquette made her acting debut at the age of eight in a production directed by her father. Her mother, Mardi, is a writer and activist in the peace movement. Arquette was raised in the heady atmosphere of 1960s-style political activism. She recalled her childhood experiences for *Rolling Stone*: "I was raised at love-ins, my mother painting STOP THE WAR on my body and us marching with Martin Luther King. Waking up in Woodstock and dancing naked." Arquette's upbringing is reflected today in her agreement with the anti-nuclear movement and her admiration for performer/activists Jane Fonda and Paul Newman.

In her early teens, Arquette lived with her parents and four younger siblings in an actors' and musicians' commune in Virginia guided by an Eastern spiritual philosophy. She left the commune at the age of thirteen when she could no longer abide the racist attitudes of her small-town high school classmates and moved by herself to New Jersey where she lived with family friends. From there, Arquette took off hitchhiking across the country. She arrived in Los Angeles

AP/Wide World Photos

at the age of seventeen and began landing parts in such television movies as "Having Babies II," "Dark Secret of Harvest Home," and "Zuma Beach." Of her early experiences in television, Arquette told *Moviegoer*, that she played "every pregnant teenage runaway hooker drug addict that was ever on the planet."

Ironically, in 1982, television also provided Arquette with the role that first brought her to the attention of critics and a larger audience. She beat out well-known actresses Mariel Hemingway, Tatum O'Neal and Diane Lane for the role of Nicole Baker in the television film "The Executioner's Song." The four-hour dramatization of the life and death of convicted murderer Gary Gilmore was adapted by Norman Mailer from his Pulitzer Prize-winning book of the same title. Actor Tommy Lee Jones starred opposite Arquette as Gilmore.

The relationship between Gilmore and Baker was the focus of the story. Described by the *New York Times* as "a spacey 20-year-old with two little children, a gallery of past husbands and boyfriends and no firm grip on anything but the pills she pops," the real life Baker met with Arquette during the filming. Arquette found it easy to identify with Baker. "When I did Nicole," Arquette told *Rolling Stone*, "I don't know how to explain it—that was the closest I ever got, I think, to actually losing it. It was so heavy being there. I love her." *People* called Arquette "stunningly right" as Baker, and Baker agreed. As Arquette told *People*: "After she saw the film she told me she loved it. 'Rosanna,' she said, 'you did me! You did me!' "

In 1983, Arquette appeared in her first starring role in a motion picture, "Baby It's You." The low-budget ($3 million) film was written and directed by independent filmmaker John Sayles. Set in Trenton, New Jersey, in 1967, the film follows its heroine, Jill Rosen, a smart, pretty, ambitious high school senior, to college at Sarah Lawrence. Along the way Jill falls for Sheik, who couldn't be a more inappropriate match for her. As Janet Maslin described the character played by Arquette, "Jill is poised, popular, a little aloof and hoping to be a star performer some day; in line with this, she stars triumphantly in a high school play and practices singing 'Stop! In the Name of Love' in front of the mirror in her bedroom." In contrast to Jill's All-American wholesomeness, Sheik, who is nicknamed for the brand of contraceptive he favors, sports slicked-back hair and shark-skin suits. He idolizes Frank Sinatra and tells Jill early in their affair that the only three people who matter are "Jesus Christ, Frank Sinatra and me."

When he cast Arquette for the role, Director Sayles told *Rolling Stone*, "I knew she was the only person who could play the innocent in the first half of the movie and bring out the emotional depth for the second part." Despite the mixed reviews the film received, critics singled out Arquette's performance for praise. According to Maslin, she played the role of Jill "crisply and confidently." *People* lauded Arquette by reporting that she "shades her performance with wonderful touches of surprise and puzzlement." In David Ansen's opinion, Arquette "makes this movie live. This seductive 23-year-old actress . . . always finds the fresh note. Like Sissy Spacek or Debra Winger, she's a presence you can't keep your eyes off, for fear of missing crucial information."

With the release of "Desperately Seeking Susan" in 1985, Arquette was included in the front ranks of young Hollywood actresses. The movie was made for $5 million, low-budgeted by Hollywood standards, and was directed by Susan Seidelman, whose previous film was the widely acclaimed "Smithereens." Described by the *Detroit Free Press* as "a stylish punk-rock version of those old '30s screwball comedies," the film features Arquette as Roberta Glass, a bored housewife in Fort Lee, New Jersey. In search of vicarious thrills, Roberta scours newspaper personal ads and becomes intrigued by a series of ads placed under the heading "Desperately Seeking Susan." Roberta begins to spy on the assignations of punk-rock star Susan and the man who places the ads. Through a number of mishaps the two women exchange identities, and Roberta gets the chance to live out her fantasy life through Susan's persona.

Real-life rock-star Madonna played the role of Susan. Although Arquette and Madonna appeared cheek-to-cheek in publicity shots and publicly professed affection and admiration for each other, press reports surfaced regarding tension between the two performers and between Arquette and Seidelman. The director attributed much of the problem

to the fact that Madonna, who was just beginning her ascent to stardom when she was hired for the part, eclipsed Arquette by the time the movie was released. "It's no secret that Rosanna and I knocked heads a lot," Seidelman told Lindsey Gruson in the *New York Times*. "She was hired to be the star. But her participation was clouded by Madonna's fast-rising star. It took the edge off her performance. People would come up to the set and say 'Madonna, Madonna, is this "The Madonna Movie?" ' Even the strongest actress would be shaken by that." For her part, Arquette told *Moviegoer* that the film was the most difficult she had ever done: "The tension on the set was unbelievable, and I hate working that way. It was a complete nightmare."

Arquette became publicly critical about the Madonna hype surrounding the release of the movie. Indeed, Orion, the distributor of the film, accelerated the release date to capitalize on Madonna's fame as a singer. Arquette also resented the fact that a video clip featuring an unreleased Madonna song, "In the Groove," was gratuitously inserted into the movie. Ultimately, Orion's ploy proved successful: The film grossed $20 million in the first three days of release, drawing a crowd largely comprised of under-21-year-old Madonna fans. Arquette told the *Detroit Free Press* somewhat ruefully, "It would be great to have Madonna fans come see it, but it would be great to have adults come see it, too."

Nor was Madonna entirely happy with the studio's strategy. She told an interviewer in *Rolling Stone*, "I have a big audience of kids for my music, and you know how they use soundtracks to push movies—I think they're using me in the same way, and it's really a drag, because I'm trying to establish myself as an actress, not as a singer making movies. But I'll be happy if it becomes a commercial success, simply because it's a different kind of movie than most of what's out now."

Arquette's experience in making her next film, the black comedy "After Hours," was much more positive. In contrast to director Seidelman's need for total control over her actors, Martin Scorsese, the director of "After Hours," was "never negative," Arquette told *Rolling Stone*. "In one situation he came up to me and said, 'Do you think you should laugh in this scene?' and I said, 'Oh no, Marty. I can't see where she'd laugh in this scene.' He said, 'Oh, yeah. You're right. You're right. Forget I ever said anything.' And he walks away. That's what he does, very subtly. It's like he planted the seed, watered it and split. And as I was doing the scene, I don't know where it came from, but I just started laughing."

The actress also enjoyed working with Director Lawrence Kasdan (who had directed "The Big Chill") in the western "Silverado." The movie is set in the 1880s, and Arquette plays a pioneer woman who crosses the continent by covered wagon. Among Arquette's other recent projects are a public television play entitled "Survival Guide" and a movie, "The Aviator," that "At the Movies" reviewer Roger Ebert called "transcendentally bad."

Arquette's personal life, once featured in the tabloids, has stabilized recently. In late 1983, Arquette took a trip to Italy and made some major decisions about the direction of her life. While her personal life was once more important to her than her career, Arquette decided to put renewed emphasis on acting. She ended her two-and-one-half year romantic relationship with Steve Porcaro, keyboardist with the rock band Toto, though they remain friends. (Arquette, as most rock fans know, was *the* Rosanna in Toto's hit song of the same name). And she entered a drug rehabilitation program. Arquette now avoids the Hollywood scene by living high above it in a rustic cabin—complete with mice, she says—in Topanga Canyon, California.

Arquette has several projects pending. She would like to do theater and is considering taking up directing. Still, her primary goal at this point in her career is to grow as an actress. To that end, she is studying with drama coach Sondra Seacat, who also coaches actress Jessica Lange. As Arquette told interviewer Dale Pollock: "I just want to work. I want to keep growing, as a human being and as an actress. *Richer* and *deeper* are definitely the words for my life right now. I'm opening doors to a lot of areas that I haven't been able to explore. I've worked from instinct a lot, now it's time to polish my technique. As an actress, I'm just a baby. I have a lot to learn."

SOURCES:

PERIODICALS

Commonweal, May 20, 1983.
Detroit Free Press, March 29, 1985.
Maclean's, November 29, 1982.
Moviegoer, April, 1985.
New York, November 8, 1982.
New York Times, March 25, 1982, October 19, 1982, November 28, 1982, June 5, 1983, April 14, 1985.
Newsweek, April 11, 1983.
People, November 29, 1982.
Rolling Stone, June 9, 1983, May 9, 1985.
Time, April 18, 1983.
Variety, February 24, 1982.
Vogue, March, 1985.
Washington Post, April 29, 1983.

—Sidelights by Barbara Welch Skaggs

Owen Beattie

BRIEF ENTRY: Canadian anthropologist. The head of a team of University of Alberta researchers, Owen Beattie captured the attention of historians, scientists, and laymen in 1984 when he disinterred three bodies preserved for 138 years in the permafrost on Canada's Beechey Island. The bodies were those of Petty Officer John Torrington, Able Seaman John Hartnell, and Royal Marine William Braine, all members of an ill-fated British expedition led by Sir John Franklin in search of the fabled Northwest Passage to China.

Franklin's expedition—the worst tragedy in the quest to find the Northwest Passage—left England with two ships and 138 men in 1845 but mysteriously disappeared. After the three sailors died and were buried on Beechey Island, the remaining explorers sailed southwest until their ships became trapped in ice near King William Island. The 105 survivors abandoned the ships the following spring, struggled to endure life on the frozen tundra, but eventually perished.

Beattie was able to account for seven of the men on King William Island, concluding in *Newsweek* that because the bones were scattered on the surface of the island, "the men literally dropped as they walked." His close examination of the bones suggested evidence of lead poisoning, scurvy, and even cannibalism. Since the three corpses unearthed on Beechey Island were in flawless condition, Beattie believes analysis of their tissue and internal organs will help determine whether it was scurvy, toxins in the food, or merely despair that killed the remaining crew. *Address:* Department of Anthropology, University of Alberta, Edmonton, Alberta, Canada.

SOURCES:

PERIODICALS

Newsweek, October 8, 1984.
Time, October 8, 1984.

Photograph by Lynda Beattie. Courtesy of Owen Beattie

Nabih Berri

1939(?)-

PERSONAL: Born c. 1939, in Freetown, Sierra Leone; son of a merchant; married wife Lila (divorced); married wife Randa; children: six (first marriage); one daughter (second marriage). *Education*: Attended Lebanese University, Beirut; graduated from Beirut Law School, 1963; also studied in France for one year.

ADDRESSES: Barbour St., Al-Nazarah, Beirut, Lebanon.

OCCUPATION: Lebanese political and religious leader.

CAREER: Worked as a merchant in family business in Sierra Leone; practiced law in Beirut, Lebanon; joined Amal political movement in Lebanon, 1974, leader of movement, 1978—; Lebanese minister of justice, 1984—. Generally recognized as leading spokesman for Lebanon's Shiite Muslims.

SIDELIGHTS: Nabih Berri is a non-traditional leader in Lebanon, a country where traditional enmities are honed and nurtured through the generations, and politicians gain ascendency by exploiting the fears of their particular religious or ethnic faction. Berri is the head of the Amal movement and leading spokesman for Lebanon's one million Shiite Muslims, the largest and most impoverished of the country's religious factions. But unlike the traditional warlords who have ruled Lebanon since World War I, Berri has tried to keep his followers on a strictly nationalistic course rather than a religious one.

"Lebanon is a country for all the Lebanese people. We are only the principle minority," he told *El Pais*, a Madrid newspaper, in 1984. In another interview, Berri told *Der Spiegel*: "Shiites demand that the existing religious system in Lebanon be abandoned. Qualifications alone, not the prayer book, should decide who becomes president of Lebanon." Another departure from the leadership of the past is Berri's disdain for any sort of personality cult. There are few posters of him to be found in West Beirut. His approach to politics is low-key and pragmatic.

Nor does Berri belong to one of Lebanon's traditional ruling families, like the Gemayels, the Jumblatts, or the Franjiehs. He is a self-made man from a middle-class background. He lives with his second wife Randa and their daughter in a modest West Beirut flat that is often described as cluttered. A favorite pastime, according to a Beirut newspaper, is watching American westerns on television. Berri was born in Freetown, Sierra Leone, where his father was a merchant; but his roots are in the south Lebanon village of Tibnin, a few miles north of the Israeli border.

He also has strong links to the United States. His first wife, Lila, lives in Dearborn, Michigan, where she works for the police department. Their six children were raised in the area.

Reuters/Bettmann Newsphotos

According to a *New York Times* profile, Berri lived in Dearborn for brief periods during the 1970s and polished his English by reading the Detroit newspapers in the Dearborn Public Library. Berri still visits his children in Dearborn and holds a U.S. government "green card," which permits him to live permanently in the United States and will eventually make him eligible for citizenship.

Berri first became involved in politics as a student at the Lebanese University in Beirut, where he was president of the student association and a member of the Baath Party, a popular pan-Arab nationalist movement of the 1960s, whose rival factions still rule in Iraq and Syria. After graduating from Beirut Law School in 1963 and studying for a year in France, Berri worked briefly with his father in Sierra Leone before returning to Beirut to practice law.

With the outbreak of the Lebanese Civil War in 1975, Berri became involved in the Amal movement, which was founded in 1974 by Shiite cleric Imam Musa Sadr as the "movement of the disinherited," an attempt to politicize Lebanon's largely passive Shiite population. When Imam Sadr disappeared during a trip to Libya in 1978—a case that has never been resolved—Berri quietly took the reins of Amal.

Lebanon's Shiites, who live primarily in and around West Beirut and in the towns and small villages of the Bekaa Valley and south Lebanon, account for about one million of the country's 3.5 million people. They are by far the largest of Lebanon's religious sects, but historically they have lagged far behind the Christian Maronites and Sunni Muslims for a fair share of Lebanon's political spoils.

Historically the Shiites broke from the orthodox Sunni Muslims during the first century of Islam in a dispute over the proper succession to the Prophet Muhammad. Over the centuries, the Shiites developed a religious outlook that is more mystical, rigid, and passionate than the Sunni. Though Sunnis predominate throughout most of the Arab world, Shiites outnumber Sunnis in Lebanon and Iraq, and significant Shiite communities live in Saudi Arabia and other Persian Gulf states. Iran (which is not an Arab state) is almost entirely Shiite.

In Lebanon, the Maronites and Sunnis profited as merchants and traders in the urban centers while the Shiites scratched a meagre existence out of the rural land in the south. But in the 1960s and 1970s, according to the *Wall Street Journal*, an economic boom in Beirut drew many Shiites to the capital, and "there they clustered in slums and seethed as they looked at their richer neighbors. Raw and illiterate, the Shiites found they didn't have access to civil service or private-sector jobs."

While it was Imam Sadr who first provided the Shiites of Lebanon with an ideological framework, it was Berri, the cool, low-key lawyer, who shaped the Amal movement into an effective political organization and maneuvered into a position where it contends for power with Maronites and Sunnis.

The turning point for Amal (which means "hope" in Arabic) came after the 1982 Israeli invasion of Lebanon. The Shiites at first welcomed the Israelis, grateful that the Palestine Liberation Organization's grip on south Lebanon had been loosened. But that gratitude was short-lived; the Shiites decided their new occupiers were no better than the old ones. Amal and a number of Shiite fundamentalist splinter groups waged an intense guerilla war, and Israel's casualties mounted steadily until it finally withdrew in June, 1985.

The more extreme of the fundamentalist groups also opposed U.S. support of the Israeli invasion as well as U.S. support of the government of Amin Gemayel, a Maronite who has been slow to make reforms. These groups took credit for the suicide car bombers that twice struck U.S. Embassy installations, a truck bomb that killed 241 U.S. Marines at their headquarters near the Beirut airport, the kidnappings of nearly a dozen American civilians since 1983, and the 1985 hijacking of a TWA jetliner.

Berri's own politics and tactics have been far more moderate. After the Israeli invasion, Berri tried to cooperate with the newly-installed Gemayel government and his American sponsors. While pressing Gemayel for reforms, he kept a tight rein on his 6,000- to 8,000-man militia until February,

1984, when Gemayel permitted the Lebanese Army to shell Beirut's predominantly Shiite southern suburbs. Berri ordered Muslim members of the Army to lay down their weapons, and within days Amal had seized effective control of West Beirut. Though this established him as the leading power in Lebanon—with even more authority than President Gemayel—few Americans had heard of Berri until June of 1985, when he emerged as a negotiator in the TWA hijacking crisis.

Despite his differences with Gemayel, Berri prefers to work for the restoration of Lebanon within a legitimate constitutional framework rather than join in the wholesale destruction of the country. He joined the government as justice minister in May, 1984, and continued to push his agenda of secular reforms. "He [Berri] is not a revolutionary by any means," a European diplomat told *The Christian Science Monitor* in 1984. "His commitment is fully to the cause of the underprivileged, which in his country means the Shiites."

When asked by *El Pais* to describe the Shiite community's goals, Berri said: "To be Lebanese on an equal footing with other Lebanese. To cease to be second-class and even third- and fourth-class citizens. And to achieve this there is only one solution: To eliminate confessionalism and secularize the country by granting posts and responsibilities on the criteria of competence and education and not religion. Note that the abolition of the confessional sharing power will continue to benefit the Christians, because the greatest number of university graduates, who will continue to hold key posts, belong to their community. But we are prepared to accept it. It is the essential condition for creating a real nation."

By early 1985, it was apparent that the real test of Berri's political acuity would come not from his rival religious factions, but from within the Shiite ranks. A number of the more militant fundamentalist groups who admire the Islamic revolution in Iran reject Berri's moderate approach. The split between Amal and fundamentalist groups such as "Islamic Amal" in the Bekaa Valley bordered on open warfare in 1985. Berri, who has tried to keep Lebanon's fundamentalists at arm's length, told *The Christian Science Monitor*: "We support the Islamic revolution in Iran, but not on sectarian grounds, and we do not want an Islamic revolution in Lebanon. Our special relations with the Iranian revolution are based more on principles than on sectarian compatibility."

Patience and moderation have never been Lebanon's strong suit. If Berri's approach does not pay dividends soon, many observers believe he may be forced to become more like the militant fundamentalists—or risk losing his following.

SOURCES:

PERIODICALS

Christian Science Monitor, February 16, 1984.
Der Spiegel (Hamburg), February 13, 1984.
Detroit Free Press, June 18, 1985.
Economist, February 11, 1984.
El Pais (Madrid), February 16, 1984.
Financial Times, February 11, 1984.

Le Monde (Paris), February 16, 1984.
London Times, February 21, 1984.
Middle East International (London), February 24, 1984.
New York Times, June 18, 1985.
Wall Street Journal, February 16, 1984, June 25, 1985.

—*Sidelights by Tom Hundley*

Willie L. Brown

1934-

PERSONAL: Full name, Willie Lewis Brown, Jr.; born March 20, 1934, in Mineola, Tex.; son of Willie Lewis (a Pullman porter) and Minnie Collins (a domestic housecleaner; maiden name, Boyd) Brown; married Blanche Vitero, 1957 (separated); children: Susan Elizabeth, Robin Elaine, Michael Elliott. *Education:* San Francisco State College (now University), B.A., 1955; Hastings College of Law, J.D., 1958. *Politics:* Democrat. *Religion:* Protestant.

ADDRESSES: Home—515 Van Ness Ave., San Francisco, Calif. 94102. *Office*—Office of the Speaker, California Assembly, State Capitol, Sacramento, Calif. 95714.

OCCUPATION: Attorney; politician.

CAREER: Admitted to the Bar of the State of California and, in 1964, to the Bar of the U.S. Supreme Court. As a youth, picked berries, peanuts, potatoes, and cotton; while in college, worked as a janitor and shoe salesman; Brown, Dearman & Smith (law firm), San Francisco, Calif., partner, 1959—; former college law instructor; California State Assembly, Sacramento, assemblyman, 1964-80, speaker of the assembly, 1980—.

Chairman of California Assembly Committee on Ways and Means, 1971-74, and of Joint Committee on Siting of Teaching Hospitals, 1973-74; vice-chairman of Select Committee on Health Manpower; member of Committee on Efficiency and Cost Control, Committee on Elections and Reapportionment, Committee on Government Administration, Governor's Committee on Aging, Joint Committee on Master Plan for Higher Education, and Select Committee on Deepwater Ports. California representative to Credentials Committee, National Democratic Convention, 1968; co-chairperson of California delegation to National Democratic Convention, 1972, and of California delegation to National Black Political Convention, 1972; delegate to Democratic National Mid-Term Conference, 1974; member of Democratic National Committee, 1977—. *Military service:* Served in U.S. National Guard.

MEMBER: National Association for the Advancement of Colored People, League of Women Voters, National Planned Parenthood Association, Chinese for Affirmative Action, San Francisco Planning and Urban Renewal Association, San Francisco Aid Retarded Children, Sunset Parkside Education and Action Committee, Fillmore Merchants and Improvement Association, Planning Association for Richmond, Haight Ashbury Neighborhood Council, Phi Alpha Delta, Alpha Phi Alpha.

AWARDS, HONORS: Outstanding Freshman Legislator Press Award, 1965; Children's Lobby Award for outstanding legislative efforts, 1974; named Leader of the Future by *Time* magazine, 1974.

UPI/Bettmann Newsphotos

SIDELIGHTS: The self-proclaimed "Ayatollah" of California government, Willie L. Brown rose from a childhood of poverty in Texas to become the first black speaker of the California Assembly and the most powerful Democrat in that state's politics in the middle eighties.

A flamboyant, eloquent, and savvy politician, Brown makes no secret of his quest for power and fame on a regional—and national—basis. As he explained to a San Francisco high school class, as quoted in the *New York Times* in 1984, "The speaker is the judge, jury and executioner in the Assembly." Brown told the *Times* that his power stems from "the ability to put numbers together, to put the appropriate number of votes together on any issue."

But others say Brown's style, as much as his legislative expertise, was instrumental in bringing him power. "Willie has great oratorical skills," fellow Democratic Assemblyman Mike Roos told *Ebony* magazine in 1984. "There's Willie, then there's everybody else. He's playing the game at a higher level than the rest."

Brown garnered national attention during the 1984 Democratic National Convention, which was held in his home town, San Francisco. He hosted a $300,000 party for 15,000 party VIPs and guests on a pier that was larger than the convention hall itself. The bash, entitled "Oh What a Night," was claimed to be the largest party in the party-loving city's history and featured ten stages for entertainers, 400 cases of California wine, and replicas of the city's most famous tourist attractions. It also solidified Brown's position as unchallenged star of California's Democratic Party. "I wanted to show people that no town can throw a party like San Francisco," Brown told the Associated Press. "And I wanted to show them that no man can throw a party like Willie Brown."

Brown is a man given to collecting $1,800 Brioni suits (his closet holds 40 of them), expensive Porsche sports cars, and saddle horses. He hobnobs with Hollywood celebrities and regularly appears in local gossip columns as an escort for attractive woman, including actress Margot Kidder. In 1984, he made *Ms.* magazine's list of the ten sexiest men in America. "If you can't wear it, drive it or make love to it," he told *Newsweek* in 1984, "I don't want it."

That same year he told *Ebony* that his opulent lifestyle enhances his image with reporters and constituents. "The media love it," he said, "I make good copy. You see, politicians are supposed to drive Fords or Chevys or Plymouths. You're expected to have a dog, three kids and a wife. You're supposed to wear white shirts and white shirts only, and wing-tip shoes. I enjoy my lifestyle and was never going to accept any of those rules. It turned out to be an incredible plus with the constituents. Most people who vote for you really don't want you to be anything but yourself. They want you to perform well and represent them well, but they do not require that you look like them or anybody else."

His rise to power did not come easily, Brown was raised in poverty in Mineola, Tex., a town of about 4,000 people outside Dallas. His father, a Pullman porter, abandoned the family when Willie was four. He and his four brothers and sisters were raised by their grandmother while their mother worked as a domestic cleaner. "I can remember using cardboard for the bottom of my shoes," he told *Ebony*. "I can remember the days of being the fourth person on the list for water for the No. 3 washtub. I remember the outdoor toilets, having to raise half of what I ate, and having meat only once a week. There's no reason why anyone should be subjected to that."

At eight, Brown worked the fields picking berries, cotton, peanuts, and potatoes. He also studied hard, he recalls, and had a vague notion of being a mathematics teacher because, he told *Ebony*. "The only groovy people I ever met or admired were math professors."

The day he graduated from Mineola Colored High School, Brown moved to San Francisco to live with an uncle, who was a gambler. Brown worked as a janitor and shoe salesman to support his way through San Francisco State College, where he first became interested in politics. In 1952, he worked on Adlai Stevenson's presidential campaign. He also joined the Young Democrats and became an officer in the local NAACP.

He calls his decision to go to law school "a total fluke." When a friend enrolled at the Hastings College of Law, Brown tagged along, wound up enrolling, and graduated as president of the class of 1958.

Brown then built a lucrative legal practice largely based on defending prostitutes and pimps. His street clientele later would be among the first contributors to his political campaigns. He told *Newsweek* that he decided to enter politics at twenty-eight when he was discriminated against while trying to buy a home in a fashionable San Francisco neighborhood. In 1962, he ran for the State Assembly against a twenty-three-year veteran and lost by 600 votes. Two years later he ran for the same seat and won.

Over the next sixteen years, Brown sponsored more than 140 bills that became California law. Among them were measures calling for tax and other financial benefits for the elderly, consumer auto insurance protection, new birth certificates for transsexuals, renter protection, improved safety for highway patrolmen, and state recognition of Martin Luther King's birthday as a legal holiday. In 1975, after seven years of trying, he convinced fellow lawmakers to pass a bill legalizing any sexual activities between consenting adults.

In 1980, on his second try, Brown was elected speaker. As presiding officer of the Assembly, he appoints all committee heads and members, allots staff and office space, has frequent and direct contact with the governor's office, controls a $40 million budget, and serves on all legislative committees. He won by forging a coalition of twenty-eight Republicans and twenty-three Democrats—ten more votes than were needed to win.

Soon after being elected, however, Republicans attacked him as overly partisan. "Willie Brown was supposed to be the reform measure," Assembly Republican leader Robert Naylor told *Newsweek.* "Obviously that didn't work." In 1984, Naylor and his GOP colleagues pushed a state ballot measure to restructure the Legislature and curtail the speaker's power. Voters approved the proposition by a fifty-three to forty-seven percent margin. But a state court knocked down the measure after Brown and other Democratic leaders filed suit, charging the changes invaded the Legislature's prerogative to set its own rules. "The streets are littered with the bleached bones of Republicans who have tried to beat Willie Brown," he boasted to the *New York Times.*

He also maintained that the ballot move—as well as other attacks on him—were basically racist in nature. "There is an unspoken conspiracy in this country to destroy blacks who move into positions of power," he told *Ebony*. "The standards for me are much higher than those for any other person who has held my spot—twice as high."

Brown claims he tries to head off such attacks by overpaying his taxes, refusing use of a state car, and sending a few hundred dollars a year to the state for use of its credit cards. Still, critics accuse him of using his legislative power for personal gain. Brown maintains a lucrative law practice, and his clients have included Neiman Marcus, Joseph E. Seagram & Sons, Southern Pacific, a Federal Reserve Bank, and major real estate developers. He told the *New York Times* that questions of conflict of interest are fair, but that "Persons I represent and the matters they ask me to support for them clearly have to be respectable. . . . My standard for myself allows me to be investigated by any authority whatsoever and walk away without a glove having been laid on Willie Brown."

In 1984, a complaint about Brown's corporate connections spurred efforts by the state's Fair Political Practices Commission to tighten up California's ethics code for lawyer-legislators. "The speaker is very effective at operating within the loopholes," FPPC Chairman Dan Stanford told *Newsweek*.

Brown continues to support controversial legislative issues. He wants to legalize the growing of up to three marijuana plants, saying it would help take the profit out of the drug trade. He would like to see casino gambling legalized in California, and in 1976 he briefly served as a hired advocate for Resorts International, the casino hotel firm.

Brown also endorses public financing of political campaigns, even though California's current system grants him great power over fundraising. Under the state's long-time policy, the speaker receives donations from individuals and groups interested in legislation and then divides the money among his supporters in the Legislature. The system allows Brown to dole out several million dollars a year, making him easily the biggest single contributor and fundraiser for state legislative candidates.

The system was designed by former Assembly Speaker Jess Unruh, the godfather of California Democrats and current state treasurer. Brown came to Sacramento in 1965 and voted against Unruh's certain re-election as speaker, thus starting his legislative career in the doghouse. But now Unruh speaks highly of Brown. "Willie's an incredibly gifted, able guy," Unruh told *Newsweek*. "Under that surface of flamboyance is a pretty good human being."

Brown gets no exercise beyond riding his horses and sleeps just three or four hours a night. His schedule is so tight, according to *Ebony*, that it is planned up to three months in advance. He has been rumored as a potential candidate for San Francisco mayor, should that job open up. He terms the post "a glamour job," comparable only to the mayoralty of New York City, but told the San Francisco *Enquirer* that he has no intention of challenging incumbent Dianne Feinstein.

Rather, he told *Ebony*, he intends to stay on as speaker: "It's important that I perform well in this position so that successive racial minorities, whether they be black, Hispanic or whatever, will be judged and treated on merit alone and nothing will be taken away from or required of them that is not required of any other person holding this office. I'm trying to break the barrier, the assumptions and the stereotypes by performing well. The system ought to be designed to create a level playing field for all of us. That's my goal."

SOURCES:

PERIODICALS

Detroit Free Press, July 16, 1984.
Ebony, April, 1981, August, 1984.
Los Angeles Times, May 27, 1984.
Ms., September, 1984.
New Republic, October 3, 1983.
New York Times, June 16, 1984, December 2, 1984.
Newsweek, August 1, 1983, June 11, 1984.
Politics Today, July 1979.
San Francisco Chronicle, July 16, 1984.
Time, December 28, 1981.
Washington Monthly, February, 1985.

—Sidelights by Glen Macnow

Marc Chagall

1887-1985

OBITUARY NOTICE: Born July 7, 1887, in Vitebsk, Russia (now U.S.S.R.); died March 28, 1985, in St. Paul de Vence, France. Russian-born Jewish artist who lived in France for almost sixty years. Chagall, whose work was characterized by vibrant colors and fanciful, dreamlike imagery, was one of the best-known and most popular artists of the twentieth century. Strongly reflective of childhood memories and religious mysticism, his paintings of floating lovers, flying animals, joyous acrobats, and vibrant flowers prompted his contemporary, Pablo Picasso, to comment that "Chagall must have an angel in his head." A *Newsweek* critic remarked at the time of Chagall's death, "If the ultimate goal of an artist is to create powerful images that permanently alter the consciousness of viewers, then no artist in this century was more successful than Chagall."

His work combined elements of a variety of artistic styles, including surrealism, impressionism, and fauvism, with the primitive qualities of his native folk art, to produce what one art critic described as a "Jewish Disneyland." In addition to his oil and watercolor paintings, which are exhibited in museums throughout the world, Chagall's *oeuvre* encompassed etchings, sculpture, lithographs, engravings, and textiles. He designed stained-glass windows depicting the twelve tribes of Israel for the Hadassah-Hebrew University Medical Center near Jerusalem, the ceiling of the Paris Opera house, murals for New York's Metropolitan Opera and Lincoln Center, and stage sets for Mozart's opera "The Magic Flute." Among Chagall's most famous paintings were *I and the Village, The Rabbi of Vitebsk*, and *The Death Man*.

On the artist's eighty-sixth birthday, the French government honored Chagall with the inauguration of a museum in Nice to house his cycle of sixty-two paintings entitled "The Biblical Message." Chagall claimed that his art relied more on inspiration than formal education and that work was his reason for living. At the age of eighty-two he said: "Work isn't to make money. You work to justify life. Those are small actions and simple truths." Several years later, Chagall explained the secret of his success: "You have to be simply honest and filled with love. When you have love, all the other qualities come by themselves."

SOURCES:

BOOKS

Alexander, Sidney, *Marc Chagall*, Cassell, 1979.

AP/Wide World Photos

Bucci, Mario, *Chagall*, Hamlyn, 1971.
The International Who's Who, 47th edition, Europa, 1983.

PERIODICALS

Chicago Tribune, March 30, 1985, April 3, 1985.
Detroit News, March 29, 1985, March 30, 1985.
Los Angeles Times, March 29, 1985.
Newsweek, April 8, 1985.
New York Times, March 29, 1985.
Time, April 8, 1985.
Washington Post, March 29, 1985.

Nicholas Colasanto

1923(?)-1985

OBITUARY NOTICE: Born c. 1923, in Providence, R.I.; died following a heart attack, February 12, 1985, in Los Angeles, Calif. Accountant, actor, and director. Colasanto was best known for his portrayal of Coach Ernie Pantusso, the endearingly befuddled bartender on the popular television series "Cheers." According to the *Chicago Tribune*, Colasanto regarded his "Cheers" character as "innocent and sweet, not dumb." His performance on that show won him two Emmy Award nominations for best supporting actor in a comedy. Prior to becoming an actor, Colasanto, then an accountant, was preparing to work for an oil company in Saudi Arabia, but when he saw a performance by Charles Boyer and Henry Fonda, he decided that he wanted to act. He pursued an acting career in New York City and subsequently appeared in dozens of television shows and in motion pictures, including "Fat City," "The Raging Bull," and Alfred Hitchcock's "Family Plot." In addition, Colasanto acted in various Broadway productions, winning a Tony Award nomination for his performance in "Across the Board Tomorrow Morning."

With the help of his friend and fellow actor, Ben Gazzara, Colasanto got his first break as a director, working on an episode of Gazzara's dramatic television series "Run for your Life." From there he went on to direct about 100 episodes of such television programs as "Bonanza," "Columbo," "Name of the Game," and "Hawaii Five-O." He had been a member of the cast of "Cheers" since its first episode in 1982. The executive producer of the show, Les Charles, told reporters: "We won't try to have another 'Coach' or anything like that character. He's irreplaceable."

AP/Wide World Photos

SOURCES:

PERIODICALS

Chicago Tribune, February 14, 1985.
Los Angeles Times, February 13, 1985.
Newsweek, February 25, 1985.
New York Times, February 14, 1985.
Time, February 25, 1985.
Washington Post, February 17, 1985.

Frederick De Cordova

1910-

PERSONAL: Full name, Frederick Timmins De Cordova; born October 27, 1910, in New York, N.Y.; son of George (in the theatre business) and Margaret (Timmins) De Cordova; married Janet Thomas, November 27, 1963. *Education:* Northwestern University, B.S., 1931; attended Harvard Law School.

ADDRESSES: Home—1875 Carla Ridge, Beverly Hills, Calif. 90210. *Office*—"The Tonight Show," National Broadcasting Co., Inc., 3000 West Alameda Ave., Burbank, Calif. 91505.

OCCUPATION: Stage, motion picture, and television producer and director.

CAREER: Shubert Enterprises, New York City, assistant to John Shubert, 1932, general stage manager, director, and producer, 1932-41; Alfred Bloomingdale Productions, New York City, general stage director, 1942; Louisville Amphitheatre, Louisville, Ky., producer, 1943; motion picture producer and director under contract to Warner Brothers, Inc., Hollywood, Calif., 1943-48, and Universal International Pictures, Hollywood, 1948-53; television producer and director, Columbia Broadcasting System (CBS), and National Broadcasting Co. (NBC), 1953—, executive producer of "The Tonight Show," NBC, 1970—.

Motion pictures produced or directed include "Too Young to Know," 1945, "That Way With Women," 1947, "Illegal Entry," 1949, "Peggy," 1950, "Bedtime for Bonzo," 1951, "Here Come the Nelsons," 1952, "Bonzo Goes to College," 1952, "I'll Take Sweden," 1965, and "Frankie and Johnny," 1966. Television series produced or directed include "December Bride," 1954-55, "The Burns and Allen Show," 1955-56, "The George Gobel Show," "The Jack Benny Program," 1960-63, "The Smothers Brothers Comedy Hour," 1965-66, and "My Three Sons."

MEMBER: Bel Air Country Club.

AWARDS, HONORS: Emmy Awards, Academy of Television Arts and Sciences, 1963, 1968, 1976, 1977, 1978, and 1979; recipient of five additional Emmy Award nominations.

SIDELIGHTS: Television producer Frederick De Cordova is a major creative force behind NBC's "The Tonight Show." While host Johnny Carson is the program's public face, De Cordova is "Tonight's" gatekeeper. With an audience of some fifteen million, an appearance on "The Tonight Show" is considered a major coup for someone with a book to sell or a movie to promote. But a would-be guest does not come near Carson without De Cordova's blessing. Once a guest is scheduled to appear, De Cordova okays the topic of conversation. And, once the show begins, he decides

AP/Wide World Photos

how long a guest chats with Carson. De Cordova also supervises the show's writing staff, monitors "Tonight's" song and dance rehearsals, and acts as Carson's majordomo. "I'm chief traffic cop, talent scout, No. 1 fan and critic all rolled into one," is how De Cordova described his job to *People* magazine. Being the chief traffic cop of "The Tonight Show," which is responsible for no less than seventeen percent of NBC's total profits, carries no small amount of clout.

When De Cordova began his stint as executive producer of "Tonight" in New York City on October 19, 1970, he was at an age when most men are planning their retirement. He celebrated his sixtieth birthday only eight days after hiring on. Until De Cordova took over, a "Tonight" executive producer had about the same longevity as a tail gunner on a World War II bomber plane. The show had seen four executive producers in eight years. But De Cordova was a show business veteran with a long resume. He had twenty-three films and some 500 television shows to his credit. In addition, he had some thirty-seven years of total entertainment business experience and was considered one of Hollywood's social lions. Fifteen years after joining the show, he still occupies the executive producer's seat.

The top five "Tonight Show" staff members (left to right): bandleader Doc Severinsen, director Bobby Quinn, host Johnny Carson, Frederick De Cordova, and second banana Ed McMahon. AP/Wide World Photos.

A native of New York City, De Cordova got his show business start as a gofer in a summer stock production in the early 1930s. De Cordova graduated from Northwestern University and made it through Harvard Law School before classmate John Shubert persuaded him to work for the Shubert entertainment empire. He spent the next ten years directing shows in Memphis, Louisville, Nashville, and New York. His last show before moving to Hollywood in 1943 was "Ziegfeld Follies," which featured Milton Berle and Arthur Treacher.

De Cordova went to Hollywood with the thought of becoming an actor but quickly abandoned the plan. As he said in an NBC press department release, "Reading some of my notices led me to become a director and producer." It wasn't until almost four decades later, when he appeared in Martin Scorcese's 1981 film "King of Comedy," that De Cordova tried acting again. After abandoning his fledgling acting career, he worked as a dialogue director in three films, "San Antonio," "Janie," and "Between Two Worlds." He made his solo directorial debut with "Too Young to Know," a 1945 effort about a career woman who was torn between a husband and a job.

De Cordova's movie career spans two periods: 1945-1953, when he directed 21 films; and 1965-1966, when he returned to film after a thirteen-year hiatus in television. Ronald Reagan, Elvis Presley, Rock Hudson, Errol Flynn, Tony Curtis, and Humphrey Bogart all appeared in De Cordova films.

The 1945-1953 period was a prolific one for De Cordova, though most of his films are known as "B" movies. He directed four films in 1951 and three movies per year in 1947, 1948, 1950, and 1952. The best-known De Cordova film, "Bedtime for Bonzo," is a 1951 comedy about a college professor who experiments with treating a chimpanzee as a child. The college professor was played by Ronald Reagan, who later was elected governor of California and then president of the United States. The movie enjoyed a revival when Reagan's political fortunes began to rise in the late 1960s. As recently as 1980, Reagan still had a sense of humor about the "Bonzo" film. In the midst of the 1980 presidential campaign, the future president autographed a reprinted studio picture of the chimp and himself in bed. The autograph read, "I'm the one with the watch." The success of the movie prompted a sequel, "Bonzo Goes to College." De Cordova directed, but Reagan did not appear. Other movies directed by De Cordova include "Little Egypt" and "Here Come the Nelsons," which featured the popular Ozzie Nelson family.

Eventually, he left the film directing business, proclaiming that he would never be another William Wyler. But he took another shot at movies in the 1960s with "I'll Take Sweden," a 1965 film that featured Bob Hope, Frankie Avalon, Tuesday Weld, and Dina Merrill. His last film was "Frankie and Johnny," which featured Elvis Presley singing saloon songs in a riverboat setting.

After abandoning his film career, De Cordova went into the infant medium of television. Among the shows he produced and directed in that period were "December Bride," "The Burns and Allen Show," "The Jack Benny Program," "The Smothers Brothers Show," and "My Three Sons." All were considered comedy classics, and he won Emmy Awards for producing "The Jack Benny Program" and for directing "The Burns and Allen Show."

"The Tonight Show," where De Cordova has worked for the last decade and a half, is a peculiar kind of American bulletin board. Host Johnny Carson engages in political satire but generally stops before he offends. As De Cordova told an Associated Press reporter, "Nothing is taboo if you do it in good taste and fun, . . . [but] when Nixon was down and out, Johnny felt that wasn't the time to zing him." The show has featured any number of writers and scientists but is not considered highbrow. It brings on movie stars and starlets regularly but isn't considered exceptionally light. As De Cordova told the Associated Press: "I try for an amalgam of guests. I don't want to see it become too Las Vegas showbizzy, or too pretentious and intellectual, either."

Other networks have tried to grab "Tonight's" audience but without much success. ABC is a good example. It used comedian Joey Bishop on late night television from 1967 until 1969. It didn't work. "The Dick Cavett Show," which ran from 1969 until 1972, was an attempt to lure an audience with a slightly more intellectual bent. That didn't

work, either. ABC's news division began its "Nightline" show in 1980, but it has still not overtaken Carson.

De Cordova monitors the flow of guests through the use of a set of three-by-five cards, which are tacked on a large corkboard behind his desk. The board tells De Cordova which guests will appear in the next 90 days. Throughout the day, De Cordova will meet with writers, consult with the show's musical director, and chat with Carson by telephone. Just before the show begins, De Cordova will assume a seat next to a camera which is only a few feet away from the host. "I like to be eyeball to eyeball with Johnny," he says. During the show's commercial breaks, he will talk with Carson about the pace of the show, the remaining guests, and the audience's reaction. Once taping is completed, he will retreat to the host's dressing room for a drink. At night, he can often be found on the Hollywood party circuit with his wife of more than twenty years, Janet. De Cordova does not often socialize with Carson, who avoids the Los Angeles party circuit.

At age 75, De Cordova shows no signs of slowing down. He is a regular on the celebrity golf circuit, and he says his vacations give him plenty of time to rest.

SOURCES:

BOOKS

Cannon, Lou, *Reagan*, Putnam, 1982.

PERIODICALS

American Film, April, 1981.
Associated Press Wire Service, July 29, 1982.
Los Angeles, August, 1981.
People, October 8, 1984.
TV Guide, January 31, 1981.

—Sidelights by Tim Kiska

Selma Diamond

1921(?)-1985

OBITUARY NOTICE: Born c. 1921, in London, Ontario, Canada; died of lung cancer, May 13, 1985, in Los Angeles, Calif. Actress and comedy writer. Diamond, who most recently appeared as Selma Hacker, the sardonic court matron on the NBC television series "Night Court," was easily recognized by her two trademarks, a gravel voice and a dangling cigarette. In addition to her acting, Diamond had been one of the few women writers during the Golden Age of Television. Beginning as a contributor to the NBC radio program "The Big Show," she became a top television writer for Perry Como, Milton Berle, and Sid Caesar. Often, she worked as part of a five-person team headed by one of the best-known comedy writers of the 1950's, Goodman Ace. Describing her experience as the only female member of that team, Diamond once said that it was "like Red China—I'm there, they just don't recognize me."

Diamond had also been the model for "The Dick Van Dyke Show" character Sally Rogers, a comedy writer played by actress Rose Marie, according to the show's creator, Carl Reiner. Reiner, who had worked with Diamond during the mid-1950's, when both were writing for "Caesar's Hour," described her comedic style as "very terse. . . . She would just walk in and drop a few plums." Diamond had been a frequent guest on television talk shows and acted in several motion pictures, including "It's a Mad, Mad, Mad, Mad World," "My Favorite Year," "Lovesick," "Twilight Zone—The Movie," and "All of Me."

SOURCES:

PERIODICALS

Chicago Tribune, May 15, 1985.
Detroit Free Press, May 14, 1985.
Newsweek, May 27, 1985.
New York Times, May 14, 1985.
Time, May 27, 1985.

AP/Wide World Photos

Terry Dolan

1950-

PERSONAL: Full name, John Terrance Dolan; born December 20, 1950, in Norwalk, Conn.; son of Joseph William and Margaret (Kelly) Dolan. *Education*: Georgetown University, B.A., 1972, LL.B., 1979. *Politics*: Conservative. *Religion*: Roman Catholic.

ADDRESSES: Home—3129 South 14th St., Arlington, Va. 22204. *Office*—1500 Wilson Blvd., Suite 513. Arlington, Va. 22204.

OCCUPATION: Political organization executive; attorney.

CAREER: Political consultant, 1972-75; National Conservative Political Action Committee (NCPAC), Arlington, Va., executive director, 1975-78, chairman, 1978—. Admitted to the bar of Washington, D.C., 1979. Chairman of Washington Legal Foundation, 1977—, and of National Conservative Foundation, 1979—; member of board of directors of Conservative National Committee and Conservatives Against Liberal Legislation.

MEMBER: American Association of Political Consultants, Americans for Nuclear Energy (treasurer), American Bar Association, Washington, D.C., Bar Association.

SIDELIGHTS: In 1980 voters were introduced to what Steven V. Roberts of the *New York Times* called "a new and highly controversial style in American politics"—the negative-image campaign, an aggressive and expensive media drive devised by New Right conservatives and aimed at liberal, primarily Democratic, candidates. Under the directorship of Terry Dolan, the National Conservative Political Action Committee (NCPAC) became one of the first and most successful organizations to employ this tactic. It targeted six key senate Democrats, depicting them as radical and out of touch with their constituents; only two of the senators won reelection. "What makes the negative campaign unusual," wrote Bernard Weinraub in the *New York Times*, "is that it seeks the defeat of the . . . incumbents without openly promoting any challengers."

NCPAC derives its strategy from a Supreme Court decision that in effect allows a political action committee (PAC) to spend unlimited amounts for or against a political cause, as long as it remains independent of any particular candidate or campaign. "The law itself was designed by liberals and labor for their own benefit," Peter Goldman and Howard Fineman of *Newsweek* explained. "But it was Dolan who married it with devastating effect to the arts of the TV spot and the direct-mail begging letter—and to his own instinct for politics as demolition derby."

Dolan entered politics in 1972 as a volunteer in Richard Nixon's reelection campaign. He joined Virginia-based NCPAC in 1975, after three years as a political consultant to

UPI/Bettmann Newsphotos

conservatives and in 1978 was promoted to chairman. Initially, NCPAC confined its efforts to raising funds "in behalf of candidates who are opposed to insane taxing policies of state and Federal Government," Dolan stated in the *New York Times*. NCPAC shifted from the role of conservative support group to that of anti-liberal crusader when Dolan and others realized that a 1976 Supreme Court decision had created a loophole in the federal election law. In 1974 the Court had restricted PACs to direct contributions of $5,000 to an individual candidate. Two years later it ruled that constitutional guarantees of freedom of speech prohibit imposing any such restriction on independent groups that do not declare support for a specific candidate. As a result, "a PAC can spend all the money it can lay hands on so long as it campaigns against a candidate without supporting his opponent," noted L. J. Davis of *Harper's*. The Court's judgment led to a proliferation of independent expenditure committees, including NCPAC.

NCPAC is considered among the most effective, ambitious, and well-organized of the independent expenditure groups, and much of its success is credited to Dolan. He first came to national attention during the 1980 senate races, when NCPAC launched a $1.2 million campaign to unseat six prominent liberal Democrats: John Culver of Iowa, Thomas Eagleton of Missouri, Frank Church of Idaho, George McGovern of South Dakota, Alan Cranston of California, and Birch Bayh of Indiana. In television, radio, and newspaper advertisements and through an extensive direct-mail campaign, the senators were attacked for their views and voting records on such issues as abortion, gun control, deficit spending, and the Equal Rights Amendment.

In Indiana, for example, voters were told that Bayh had supported $46 billion in deficit spending. Showing a large sausage in the background, the NCPAC commercial charged that "one very big piece of baloney is Birch Bayh telling us he's fighting inflation." Another television spot, viewed by South Dakotans, featured a basketball player dribbling a ball while an announcer stated, "Globetrotter is a great name for a basketball team, but it's a terrible name for a senator." The voice-over continued: "While the energy crisis was brewing, George McGovern was touring Cuba with Fidel Castro. He also took a one-month junket to Africa. All at the taxpayer's expense. No wonder he lost touch with South Dakota. With so many problems at home, we need a senator and not a globetrotter." After the elections only Cranston and Eagleton retained their senate seats. Most political analysts agree that NCPAC efforts greatly contributed to the defeat of the other four.

In 1982 Dolan and NCPAC met with far less success. There were fewer big-name Democrats up for reelection, and those who were—Edward Kennedy of Massachusetts, Patrick Moynihan of New York, and Paul Sarbanes of Maryland—represented traditionally liberal constituencies. In addition, Roberts observed that "the current power of conservatives has forced some liberals to drift rightward, and their shift has defused some of [NCPAC's] arsenal."

While the political climate favored conservative candidates, economic conditions did not. The country was in the midst of a recession, which many Americans blamed on the policies of Republicans, especially Ronald Reagan. Dolan himself attributed the conservatives' setback to the president, but for a different reason. He contends that Reagan has been influenced by White House moderates and liberals and has abandoned the conservative agenda. "We're on the defensive largely because of the initiatives of the Reagan Administration," Dolan told David Shribman of the *New York Times*. "Everything played into our hands in 1980. Not any more. We have a President who talks about arms freezes, we have a President who prepares $100 billion budget deficits. We have a President backing away from much of the coalition that elected him."

Roberts, however, believes that NCPAC "has been hampered by its own success." He explains that "potential victims are now forewarned, and forearmed, the element of surprise has been lost." Several senators targeted by NCPAC in 1982, for instance, embarked early on their campaigns. And according to Goldman and Fineman, NCPAC's previous triumphs "inspired an alphabet soup of new liberal PACs to plagiarize its hit-and-run tactics and turn them on NCPAC and its conservative friends, quite literally with a vengeance." Meanwhile, Republicans worried that Dolan's negative approach could backfire. "The Massachusetts Republican leadership invited them to stay away, for fear that a NCPAC attack would only martyr

Teddy [Kennedy]—not defeat him," Goldman and Fineman maintained. "Even GOP National Chairman Richard Richards, a handpicked Reagan man, accused NCPAC of making 'all kinds of mischief.' The charge stung the committee, seeming as it did to signal the President's own displeasure."

The rift between Dolan and the Republican party continues. Dolan views NCPAC as the "conscience, the cutting edge" of the conservative effort, he told Roberts. "We've never been in the mold of respectable, establishment Republicans, and we don't want to be." In 1983 Dolan again accused the president of deserting the conservative program. John Dillin of the *Christian Science Monitor* wrote: "[Dolan] says that Reagan was elected on 'the most conservative platform in modern history' and then 'surrendered' everything after getting into office. Why? It's all the product of 'savvy White House pragmatists'—who are 'the same people Reagan defeated in 1980.' " Dillin noted that many Reagan policies, such as tax and spending cuts, a strong defense, and business deregulation, "reflect essentially traditional Republicanism." What angers Dolan and other conservatives is Reagan's failure to "harness the American voters' 'moral outrage' " on several issues, among them forced busing, abortion, Soviet troops in Afghanistan, and the Soviet Union's alleged use of chemical warfare. "Conservatives call this a mistake," stated Dillin. "Such issues . . . could be a powerful force turning middle-class Americans toward conservative (Republican) candidates."

Dolan's disillusionment with the GOP seemingly reached its peak in the summer of 1984, when he announced that he would resign as chairman of NCPAC to help organize the Conservative Populist party. Shortly thereafter, he addressed an unauthorized, pre-convention platform hearing called by liberal Republicans, who feared that the party's official platform would be unduly influenced by the New Right and would cost the president votes. Dolan told the assemblage that it could "help the Republican party by leaving it," the *New York Times* reported. He termed the meeting "a cheap media stunt" and added: "Since I am myself not adverse to cheap media stunts, I want to congratulate you for coming up with one of the cheapest of all, a bunch of senators largely ignored by their party because they act as if they are members of the other party giving advice on how their party should conduct itself. If the media buys this, they will buy anything."

Dolan's critics agree that he is "not adverse to cheap media stunts," and worse. As head of NCPAC Dolan has been branded an extremist and a liar; his methods have been denounced as unfair, exploitative, and a threat to democracy. Many observers maintain that there is some truth to these charges. "In Idaho, Church was criticized for his strong attacks on the CIA, which was fair enough," commented *Time*'s Edwin Warner, "but he was also falsely accused of disclosing the names of CIA agents and thereby putting their lives in danger." A television commercial, also against Church, "showed an abandoned missile silo, making the point that he had voted against military programs," Warner continued. "In fact, the Air Force had removed the missile because it was outdated, and Church had voted in favor of the weapon's replacement."

NCPAC's sometimes slanted advertisements are not all that disturb its critics. They argue that the organization evades campaign finance laws by claiming independence. "The key to Dolan's continued success lies in his remaining 'independent' of the candidate whose cause he is aiding," asserted *New York*'s Michael Kramer. "Prove Dolan isn't independent and you destroy his effectiveness. But, as Dolan gleefully pointed out, 'no one can rationally define independence—it's a ridiculous concept.'"

During the 1982 New York senate race between incumbent Democrat Patrick Moynihan and Republican challenger Bruce Caputo, for example, NCPAC ran a series of commercials attacking the former while disavowing any direct ties to the latter. However, "Moynihan boosters point to strong overlaps between [NCPAC] and the Caputo campaign," the *New York Times* reported. "Both employ the same political consultant. [NCPAC] has already provided $4,400 to Mr. Caputo, apart from the much larger sums its anti-Moynihan advertising will require." Moynihan's response, said Kramer, was that Dolan is "manifestly violating the law's intent. The connection between Dolan and Caputo is clear. To believe otherwise requires a degree of innocence unattainable in our time."

According to Kramer, Dolan has called the election statute "a stupid law." Moreover, he has acknowledged that "groups like ours are potentially very dangerous to the political process." Dolan further explained: "Ten independent expenditure groups, for example, could amass this great amount of money and defeat the point of accountability in politics. We could say anything we want about an opponent of Senator Smith, and the senator wouldn't have to say anything. . . . A group like ours could lie through its teeth, and the candidate it helps stays clean."

Dolan made these remarks, Goldman and Fineman pointed out, in an argument for election law reform. They noted that "even as he defends his work, [Dolan] laments the anomalies in the election-finance law that make 'independent' political commandos like NCPAC possible." In fact, a number of suits seeking to block the efforts of NCPAC and other independent expenditure committees have been filed. The Federal Elections Commission and the Federal Communications Commission have heard similar complaints. So far, rulings have been in favor of the independent organizations.

Dolan concedes that NCPAC's activities take advantage of a legal loophole, but he insists that, with few exceptions, the group's advertisements are accurate and carefully researched. He freely admits that NCPAC's negative image strategy is perceived as less than estimable. According to Weinraub, Dolan admits that "there's no question about it—

we are a negative organization. . . . We're interested in ideology. We're not interested in respectability. We're going to . . . send a shiver down the spine of every . . . liberal Senator and Congressman." Dolan further stated: "Images are important, not issues. . . . Start with an image like George McGovern doesn't represent South Dakota. Keep hitting away. That's more effective than George McGovern did or didn't do X, Y or Z for South Dakota." Michael Malbin, a political scientist with the American Enterprise Institute, told the *Newsweek* reporters that "in some ways" negative campaign advertising is "an improvement on what was popular in the 1970's—all those ads showing a guy walking on a beach with a coat over his shoulder."

Dolan and others contend that the anger directed at NCPAC stems from ideological rather than ethical concerns. The *National Review*'s William F. Buckley, Jr., stated that Dolan is "both philosophical and shrewd. He says simply that, if the voters are informed, but want in any event to go with a particular candidate, why let them do so. Shrewd, too, in divining that the general furor results less from the circulation of information by [NCPAC] than by its ideological predisposition. How many people have denounced the labor unions' political action committees, or those representing civil rights, or ecology, or the interests of education, or of the aged?" In examining the 1980 elections, Warner found that NCPAC was most concerned with familiarizing voters with their representatives' performances. "N.C.P.A.C.'s main object was to expose the incumbent's voting record for the citizens back home," he wrote. "The Senators tended to vote to the left of their constituents while playing down this fact in their campaigns." Conservative activist Richard Viguerie's summation, according to Warner, is that "N.C.P.A.C. went up to the doorstep and left the dead cats."

SOURCES:

PERIODICALS

Christian Science Monitor, May 23, 1983, December 22, 1983.
Harper's, October, 1980.
National Review, May 15, 1981.
Newsweek, June 1, 1981.
New York, December 14, 1981.
New York Times, November 2, 1975, October 28, 1976, August 17, 1979, March 24, 1980, October 5, 1980, November 18, 1981, January 14, 1982, July 27, 1982, August 17, 1982, August 30, 1982, September 6, 1982, June 4, 1984, July 31, 1984.
Time, December 8, 1980.

—Sketch by Denise Wiloch

Angelo R. Donghia

1935-1985

OBITUARY NOTICE: Born March 7, 1935, in Vandergrift, Pa.; died of pneumonia, April 10, 1985, in New York, N.Y. Interior designer and businessman. Considered one of America's most influential interior designers, Angelo R. Donghia was noted for his bold, contemporary approach to home and commercial furnishings. Some of his style innovations—gray flannel upholstery on over-stuffed furniture, shiny lacquered walls, and bleached wood floors—have become contemporary design standards. In addition to homes, Donghia decorated restaurants, hotels, corporate offices, and clubs. His clients and commissions included Mary Tyler Moore, Neil Simon, Halston, PepsiCo, Miami's Omni International Hotel, and the Metropolitan Opera Club.

Donghia decided to become a designer as a child, and he subsequently attended Parsons School of Design. Upon graduation in 1959, he joined New York's prestigious Yale Burge Interiors. He became the firm's vice-president in 1963 and a partner in 1966. In 1968 Donghia founded & Vice Versa, a trend-setting fabric and wall-covering company. His first showroom opened in Los Angeles in 1976. Two years later he established Donghia Furniture. Donghia was one of the first decorators to successfully mass-market designer products, and through Donghia Companies he promoted his own line of glassware, china, sheets, fabrics, wallpaper, and furniture.

SOURCES:

PERIODICALS

Chicago Tribune, April 14, 1985.
Newsweek, April 22, 1985.
New York Times, April 12, 1985.
Time, April 22, 1985.

Fred R. Conrad/NYT Pictures

Elmer W. Engstrom

1901-1984

OBITUARY NOTICE: Born August 25, 1901, in Minneapolis, Minn.; died October 30, 1984, in Hightstown, N.J. American electronics executive. Engstrom worked for the RCA Corporation for 41 years, serving as president between 1961 and 1965. He played a major role in RCA's development of the world's first color television tube. Other products developed under Engstrom's supervision include equipment for sound motion pictures and broadcasting receivers.

After graduating from the University of Minnesota in 1923, Engstrom joined the Radio Engineering Department of the General Electric Company. When GE's radio and engineering activities were transferred to RCA in 1930, Engstrom became a division engineer. For the next 25 years, he served in various research capacities at RCA. He directed the company's television research and development efforts for several years and eventually headed RCA's development of the first color television system. When, in 1942, RCA consolidated all of its research efforts in Princeton, N.J., Engstrom was named director of general research. From that position he graduated to vice-president, executive vice-president, senior executive vice-president, and finally, in 1961, to president. When he was presented with the Founders Award of the Institute of Electrical and Electronics Engineers in 1966, Engstrom was cited for "his foresighted application of systems engineering concepts in bringing television to the public." Engstrom retired from RCA in 1971.

SOURCES:

BOOKS

The International Who's Who, 1980-81, Europa, 1980.

PERIODICALS

New York Times, November 2, 1984.

AP/Wide World Photos

Sam Ervin

1896-1985

OBITUARY NOTICE: Full name, Samuel J. Ervin, Jr.; born September 27, 1896, in Morganton, N.C.; died of respiratory and kidney failure, April 23, 1985, in Winston-Salem, N.C. Politician, lawyer, judge, lecturer, and author. A United States senator for twenty years, Sam Ervin is best remembered for his role in the 1973 Watergate hearings. As Democratic chairman of the Senate Select Committee on Presidential Campaign Activities, Ervin presided over the investigation that eventually led to Richard Nixon's resignation. Ervin, who described himself as "just an ol' country lawyer," became the hero of Watergate, an event he considered "the greatest tragedy this country has ever suffered." Throughout the widely televised hearings, Ervin displayed indignation, persistence, down-home common sense, and humor. His approach "helped reassure Americans that there were still people in Washington with moral bearings solidly fixed," recalled Kurt Andersen of *Time*.

The son of a lawyer, Ervin attended the University of North Carolina then served eighteen months in France during World War I. He was twice wounded and twice cited for gallantry in battle. After the war he earned a degree from Harvard Law School. He returned to North Carolina to practice law and to pursue a political career. In 1925 Ervin was elected to the North Carolina General Assembly. He became a county judge ten years later and a superior court judge in 1937, and he was named to the North Carolina Supreme Court in 1948. Ervin joined the U.S. Senate in 1954.

Although he championed a number of liberal causes, such as the censuring of Senator Joseph McCarthy and the fight to block a government-proposed citizen surveillance system, Ervin was considered a staunchly conservative southern Democrat. He opposed most civil rights legislation and the Equal Rights Amendment; he was against giving eighteen-year-olds the right to vote. He strongly supported the Vietnam War, and he generally favored business over labor in legislative disputes. A states' rights advocate, Ervin revered the U.S. Constitution, which, he said, "should be taken like mountain whiskey—undiluted and untaxed," *Newsweek* reported. His colleagues regarded him as the Senate's foremost authority on the document. Ervin retired from the Senate in 1974, shortly after the Watergate

UPI/Bettmann Newsphotos

investigation. He spent his later years practicing law in his home state, lecturing, and writing. Ervin's account of the Watergate hearings, *The Whole Truth*, was published by Random House in 1981.

SOURCES:

PERIODICALS

Detroit Free Press, April 24 1985.
Newsweek, May 6, 1985.
Time, May 6, 1985.

Nanette Falkenberg

1951-

PERSONAL: Born April 27, 1951, in Scranton, Pa.; daughter of a small business owner. *Education*: Bucknell University, B.A., 1973.

ADDRESSES: Office—National Abortion Rights Action League, 1424 K St. N.W., Washington, D.C. 20005.

OCCUPATION: Social activist; political organizer.

CAREER: Senate campaign worker in Nevada and Oregon prior to 1973; AFL-CIO, American Federation of State, County and Municipal Employees (AFSCME), union organizer, beginning 1973, associate director of political action, beginning 1979, liason to National Democratic Party; currently executive director of National Abortion Rights Action League, Washington, D.C.

MEMBER: Phi Beta Kappa.

SIDELIGHTS: In the arena of women's issues—a political realm filled with outspoken feminist authors, born-again ministers, and controversial politicians of all stripes—Nanette Falkenberg is something of a surprise. She describes herself as a hard-headed, no-nonsense political strategist for the cause of legal, accessible abortions for every woman who wants one. In this way, she cuts a figure that is often quite at odds with others in the emotionally charged war being waged over abortions in the United States.

AP/Wide World Photos

This soft-spoken, articulate woman is *the* national spokesman for abortion rights in this country. She appears on talk shows—often squaring off against a fundamentalist minister or Catholic priest or anti-abortion housewife. She is frequently contacted by news magazines for her views on some new development, be it the rash of bombings of abortion clinics or some unexpected turn in the legislative effort for a constitutional amendment to ban abortions. She and her organization, the National Abortion Rights Action League (NARAL), counter nearly every major anti-abortion pronouncement with their own news releases and public statements, in order to give their position on abortion the widest possible currency.

In the eighties, as the battle over abortions is waged in the legislatures and in the courts, Nanette Falkenberg is likely to be the single most influential "pro-choice" figure on the national scene. Since the future of legal, accessible abortions is now in question, especially if President Reagan chooses to appoint anti-abortion justices to the Supreme Court and other federal benches, Falkenberg and NARAL will have their hands full in their efforts. Indeed, the availability of abortions in this country may come down to just how effective a political strategist Falkenberg is.

She appears to be up to the job. Although she has been a supporter of legal, accessible abortions throughout her life, she was hired as executive director by NARAL for her political skills, largely gained as a worker on political campaigns, as a union organizer and political strategist for union interests. Even now Falkenberg prefers to think of herself as a strategist more than a "pro-choice" ideologue. She says no heart-rending personal experiences molded her stand on abortion. "I don't think I came to this job because of any personal experiences," she told CN, but "because of my personal potential to create political influence" on behalf of the pro-choice cause.

Falkenberg has been busy creating this influence throughout much of her life. Born in 1951, the only child of a small businessman in Scranton, Pennsylvania, she attended public schools there and, later, Bucknell University. During college, she briefly considered becoming a lawyer, a profession that would certainly have been suited to her predilection for rational analysis over histrionics and emotionalism. But while still a student, working on the George McGovern campaign in 1972, Falkenberg was smitten by politics and thereafter would never really separate herself from this area. She graduated Phi Beta Kappa in political science from

Bucknell in 1973, worked on senate campaigns in Nevada and Oregon, and then was hired, in 1975, as union organizer for the American Federation of State, County and Municipal Employees, a branch of the AFL-CIO. "I did a lot of straight union organizing there," Falkenberg recalls. But she soon gravitated to work that was more clearly "political," rising through the ranks to become associate director of political action in 1979. Her job then was to coordinate AFSCME efforts on behalf of sympathetic candidates in the state and municipal campaigns. She also served as the union's liaison to the National Democratic party.

Though hired by NARAL more for her skills than for her ideology, Falkenberg could hardly be called a political mercenary. She has invariably worked for causes that she believed in. On the abortion issue, Falkenberg maintains that the whole question is not as black and white as the anti-abortionists contend, and her stance is this: Since there is no agreement on exactly when human life begins, a decision on whether to have an abortion should be made by the pregnant woman. "And while there is no consensus on when life begins" she explained to *CN*, "there is a very clear consensus among the American people that the decision on abortion ought to be left to the individual woman. . . . And I think the strength of that position is that, if an individual believes that life begins at conception, and that it would be difficult if not impossible for her to have an abortion, then she can choose not to have one."

Ms. Falkenberg has said repeatedly that, if abortions were made illegal in this country, abortions would still be common, and widespread flouting of the laws would take place. She does favor better birth-control education in this country to diminish the number of abortions performed each year but points out that even the most effective birth control means, the oral contraceptive, is only 98 percent effective. "Even if every woman used the pill, there would still be 200,000 unwanted pregnancies each year from pill failures."

Obviously, the one thing that Falkenberg and NARAL would least like to see is a ban on abortions. The organization remembers the time of illegal abortions all too clearly. NARAL itself has its roots in an organization, the National Association for the Repeal of Abortion Laws, that was founded in 1969, four years before the Supreme Court made abortion legal in its historic *Roe vs. Wade* decision. Since 1973, the renamed organization has endeavored not only to keep abortions legal, but also to make them accessible to all women, even very poor ones. This has meant lobbying at the level of state legislatures for financing of abortions for welfare recipients and the indigent. The organization also lobbies members of Congress, makes campaign endorsements, and provides some funding of the campaigns of candidates sympathetic to their cause. In the 1982 presidential election year, spending totalled $700,000.

NARAL therefore plays a preponderant role in the pro-choice battle. It is the only national organization whose sole purpose is assuring what it considers to be the abortion rights of women, although it has some allies in this task: the National Organization for Women, Planned Parenthood, and the American Civil Liberties Union. NARAL's opponents include Right to Life, an anti-abortion group, the hierarchy of the Roman Catholic church, the Moral Majority, and President Ronald Reagan, who favors a ban on all abortions, except those undertaken to save the life of the mother. Statements in NARAL literature have termed the president's positions on abortion-related issues—especially his decision to have the firearms and tobacco enforcement agency and not the FBI investigate bombings at abortion clinics—as "callous" and "dangerous."

Within NARAL, Falkenberg's role is that of spokesperson and strategist. She says she especially enjoys working out the broad outlines of NARAL strategy. "I'm not a detail person. I delegate. I'm learning to delegate," she told *CN*. One priority is building up the organization's membership, and Falkenberg says she is proud of the fact that the number of NARAL members has just topped 200,000 nationwide. (She indicates that one of the reasons that she was hired in 1981 was to add members to the group as effectively as she did as a union organizer for AFSCME.) During the recruiting of volunteers, trained NARAL speakers hold informal meetings in private homes. Once on board, the members perform tasks such as compiling lists of pro-choice individuals and then, in turn, recruiting them for letter-writing campaigns, fund-raising, and other activities.

Another important activity is lobbying. Falkenberg says her greatest accomplishment since joining NARAL was the recent campaign to convince legislators that a pro-choice stance on abortion does not hurt them at the polls—something NARAL says was proven in the 1984 state and national elections. "I think on the hard political stuff, we have done very well," Falkenberg says. "The people's inclination in this country, after all, has been pro-choice, and I think we have helped political candidates learn about this." Another lobbying function is the training of grassroots members to lobby for abortion rights on the state and local level.

In mid-1985, however, NARAL went on the defensive in the battle for U.S. public opinion when Dr. Bernard Nathanson, an ex-abortionist who had a change of conviction, produced the anti-abortion movie "Silent Scream," a sonogram of a fetus being aborted that quickly garnered national publicity for his cause. Falkenberg and NARAL responded on an equally emotional level. A new ten-week, $200,000 campaign was mounted to show that women with unwanted pregnancies are victims, too. Thousands of women were urged to "go public" and tell the story of their decision to have an abortion. The campaign marked a shift in the pro-choice effort, especially for Falkenberg. "We [previously] had a conscious desire to de-emotionalize the issue," she told *CN*, "and I don't think that we can play it that way anymore. . . . We have to say, 'You want emotion, we'll give you emotion.'"

Even with this response, the film had clearly taken its toll. Falkenberg was disturbed by the fact that "Silent Scream" showed the fetus, but not the mother who had chosen to have an abortion. At one point, according to *Boston Globe* columnist Ellen Goodman, Falkenberg asked a reporter in a burst of frustration, "Do you think the fetus is housed in a Tupperware jar?" The debate over "Silent Scream" was clearly taking the abortion debate in a direction that Falkenberg did not want it to go. "We won't fight the fetus fight with them," Falkenberg later told Goodman. "Instead we want to remind people that the fetus is carried by a living, breathing, thinking woman."

But the biggest test of Ms. Falkenberg's political savvy may be yet to come: Twenty-nine states have proposed legislation to ban or restrict abortions, and demonstrations and even violence have begun erupting at many abortion clinics. Worst of all for the pro-choice movement, President Reagan may soon have the opportunity to appoint new justices to the U.S. Supreme Court—the body that made abortions legal in the first place. At last count, six of the nine justices agreed with the 1973 decision, but five justices are over seventy-five and may soon retire. Thus, by virtue of his powers to appoint them, Mr. Reagan may soon have the opportunity to shape judicial opinion on abortion for the next forty years. It is not a prospect that Falkenberg and NARAL relish.

SOURCES:

PERIODICALS

Boston Globe, January 31, 1985.
Ms., August, 1982.
New York Times, June 12, 1983, June 6, 1984, January 12, 1985.

—Sidelights by Gary Hoffman

Trevor Ferrell

1972-

BRIEF ENTRY: Born 1972, in Gladwyne, Pa. American youth, whose campaign to aid Philadelphia's homeless has received national attention. Trevor Ferrell's self-described "mission" began in December of 1983 when he saw a television news report on the city's street people. Shocked at the sight, he asked his parents if the problem was as serious as the report stated. His father, a successful businessman, volunteered to show him firsthand. Young Ferrell brought along a blanket and pillow, which he gave to a man lying on a subway grate. Since that night the family has regularly returned, bringing coffee, hot meals, and clothing.

Ferrell's efforts were first reported by suburban newspapers and local television stations; soon the national media picked up the story. Public reaction has been overwhelming. The Ferrells have received nearly $50,000 in contributions. Churches, synagogues, men's clubs, restaurants, and super-markets have donated various goods and services. New Jersey's Fort Dix Army Training Center sent one hundred surplus overcoats. A Volkswagen van and a thirty-room boarding house have also been donated. The Ferrell family has received several awards, plaques, and city council commendations, and they have been approached by movie companies and book publishers eager to tell their story.

In spite of public support and official praise, the Ferrells find it increasingly difficult to maintain their operation. Trevor's father, Frank, temporarily closed his electronics sales and service business to work full time on his son's campaign. The family has exhausted its savings and now depends on their church and friends for financial support. Moreover, Trevor's mother, Janet, was attacked by a street person in 1984. The family remains devoted to the project, however, and they are not without hope. Resources for Human Development, a nonprofit organization, is furthering their cause, and they continue to receive contributions from across the country.

Young Ferrell refers to Philadelphia's homeless as "my friends." They, in turn, call him "little buddy," "John Boy," and "little Jesus." *McCall's* writer Maryann Bucknum Brinley comments: "He never judges the street people for their inability to make a living wage or to stay sober. All he wants to do is help. When the first man lying on the grate

AP/Wide World Photos

said, 'God bless you,' thanking him for the blanket, [his mother explains,] 'Trevor couldn't wait to do it again.' "
Address: Trevor's Campaign, Resources for Human Development, 120 West Lancaster Ave., Ardmore, Pa. 19003.

SOURCES:

PERIODICALS

McCall's, January, 1985.
New York Times, March 12, 1984.
People, March 26, 1984, December 24, 1984.

Kirk Gibson

1957-

PERSONAL: Full name, Kirk Harold Gibson; born May 28, 1957, in Pontiac, Mich.; son of Robert (a tax auditor and high school mathematics teacher) and Barbara (a high school theater and speech teacher) Gibson. *Education:* Attended Michigan State University, 1975-78.

ADDRESSES: Home—Grosse Pointe, Mich. *Office*—Detroit Tigers Baseball Club, Tiger Stadium, Michigan and Trumbull, Detroit, Mich. 48216.

OCCUPATION: Professional baseball player.

CAREER: Baseball player in minor leagues, 1978-79, and in major leagues with Detroit Tigers, 1979—.

SIDELIGHTS: Baseball player Kirk Gibson of the Detroit Tigers made a major impression on the American sports scene during the final game of the 1984 World Series, when he hit two home runs to lead his team to an 8-4 victory over the San Diego Padres, the final victory in a five-game Series triumph. After circling the bases for the second time that dark, cool, misty Sunday afternoon, the 6-foot, 3-inch, 215-pound Gibson—his heavily-whiskered face beaming with joy and his shaggy blond hair blowing freely from his hatless head—ran toward the Tiger dugout and thrust his clenched fists skyward while more than 50,000 Detroit fans cheered and the cameras from national television and print media captured the moment.

For the 27-year-old Gibson, the triumphant scene on the national stage marked a high point in a baseball career that has been at times successful, at times frustrating, and often controversial. The pose seemed to sum up all the fury and ability within him. "I may not be the next (Mickey) Mantle," he told *Sports Illustrated,* "But I'll tell you one thing: I'll be remembered."

The next year, the 1985 baseball season, was to be a pivotal year in his career. Unable to come to terms with the Tigers on a long-term contract, Gibson signed for one year at a salary of $675,000. While that wage is higher than that paid most American workers, it is modest for baseball stars, some of whom make between $1 million and $2 million per year on long-term contracts. Before the 1985 season, Gibson announced that he would not negotiate with the Tigers during the playing season and that he intended to make himself available for baseball's free-agent draft before the 1986 season.

The free-agent draft, for veteran players, is an annual process by which some players change teams after choosing among bids from teams drafting them. For Gibson, who had played only with Detroit in the major leagues, the decision was a major step not without risk. Although touted for years for his potential and although he had been outstanding in

Photograph by Kathy Marcaccio

1984, he had not—up until that point—been able to put together two consecutive successful baseball seasons.

In 1983, for instance, Gibson batted a weak .227 and was frequently booed by the hometown fans. "He was booed mercilessly," a *Sports Illustrated* reporter wrote. "There were rumors about booze, broads and drugs, the three deadly sins of professional sport. His response to the acrimony was to lose his temper in public and private. . . . " Gibson agrees: "I had vendettas out against the fans, the press, everybody." After his performance in the World Series finale—which included five runs batted in and scoring the winning run with a dash from third base to home plate—Gibson told the *New York Times,* "I don't want to dwell on the bad times, they're behind me now."

Born in Pontiac, Michigan, on May 28, 1957, and raised in the northern Detroit suburb of Waterford, Gibson was a football star from 1975 through 1978 at Michigan State University, where he earned All-America honors as a flanker who caught forward passes. In his four seasons with the Spartans, he set MSU records with 112 catches, 2,347 yards and 24 touchdown receptions. Football scouts believed him to be a sure bet as a pro star, and Gibson was drafted by the St. Louis Cardinals football team as well as by the Tigers. But instead of football, Gibson chose baseball, where careers are often longer and higher-paying, even though he had played only one year of baseball at the college level.

An intense, strong-willed and competitive person, Gibson played less than two seasons in the Detroit minor league system before breaking in with the Tigers in September of 1979. Jack Billingham, a Detroit pitcher at the time, recalled Gibson's tense mood before that 1979 debut in an interview published in the *Detroit Free Press*. Gibson was undergoing a pre-game trainer's massage in the team's Tiger Stadium medical room when Billingham, a veteran, began to tease the rookie. "I was saying 'What's the matter, you nervous?' and he didn't even smile," Billingham said. "He yells, 'Jack, just leave me alone, just leave me alone' and I saw a look in his eyes of fire, so I stopped. . . . Fifteen or 20 minutes later, I'm going through those swinging doors of the trainer's room and he comes walking through again and I say 'Geez, you can't stay out of there, can you?' And he comes at me with a flying body block, knocks me 10 feet! I don't think it's too funny to have an ex-football player charge me. I was no fool, so I stayed away from him after that. But I said 'Relax,

Kirk. If you're going to play this game and you stay that tense, you're gonna go crazy.' "

In the following years, Gibson developed a reputation for dramatic clutch hitting, dramatic batting slumps and demonstrative temper tantrums. He missed more than half of the 1980 and 1982 seasons with wrist injuries. When he was healthy and playing—and even when injured—he was a very visible star in his home town and he became known for his visits to nightclubs and bars. Fans in Detroit occasionally complained of his reluctance to sign autographs. Gossip columnists and other reporters on Detroit's major newspapers published stories about Gibson's public behavior, which often included loud cursing.

Stories chronicled, among other things, his snub of a retarded child who requested an autograph when Gibson was injured and out of uniform at Tiger Stadium and his failure to show for a promised appearance at a Christmas party for a Detroit-area orphanage. In 1984, even while en route to the best season of his career, he stormed out of Tiger Stadium after a frustrating game, started up his red Jeep Renegade and tried to get home ahead of heavy traffic. Instead, he crashed into another vehicle. And after the World Series victory parade in downtown Detroit, when

As San Diego Padres catcher Terry Kennedy (left) looks on, Kirk Gibson hits a two-run homer at Tiger Stadium in the first inning of the fifth and final game of the World Series, October 14, 1984. AP/Wide World Photos.

Gibson and teammate Dave Rozema were driving home to suburban Grosse Pointe, their vehicle overturned after an accident with another car.

"The basic way I've changed is I'm much more rational now," Gibson said in an interview with *Monthly Detroit* magazine. "Hey, lookit—I did a lot of stupid, irrational things. I admit it. I did some embarrassing things. I was like push-pull. It's called the low low concept. Lock on, lock out. But to grow, you have to learn by your mistakes. I used to have too big an ego and I know I'm a very arrogant person. But now I know why I do what I do, and I know what I want and I'm going to succeed."

In 1984—with no injuries, 149 games played, 27 home runs, 91 runs batted in, and a batting average of .282—Gibson obviously enjoyed the most successful season in his first six. But in the previous years, he had shown dramatic flashes of talent. Two of the most remarkable episodes came on June 14, 1983, in a game at Tiger Stadium against the Boston Red Sox. Early in the game, Gibson hit a home run that cleared not only the right-field fence but also the right-field grandstand and stadium roof. It landed outside the ball park, on the roof of a building across the street. It was later estimated that the ball traveled 540 feet.

That feat alone made for a remarkable performance, but Gibson wasn't finished. Later in the game, he hit a ball over the head of Boston center fielder Tony Armas. The ball bounced off Armas's glove and hit the center field wall 440 feet from home plate, the deepest part of the playing field. Tiger teammate Lou Whitaker, who started the play at first base, was tagged out at the plate by catcher Rich Gedman. When home plate umpire Larry Barnett stated to signal Whitaker out, he was knocked to the ground by Gibson, who unexpectedly had caught up almost behind Whitaker and had continued on to the crowded scene at home plate. "I was chasing Lou home and I was going to try to jar the ball loose," Gibson said after the game. "It was a great relay, and I was surprised the ball was there. Hell, I was out by 10 feet. I figured my only chance was to try and plow him [Gedman] over." The collision knocked the umpire unconscious. First base umpire Ken Kaiser had to make a ruling on the play, so he called Whitaker "out" and Gibson "safe."

Skilled in more than one sport, Gibson at times inspires admiration in men of other athletic professions. On May 10, 1985, he hit a ball over the roof in right field at Chicago's Comiskey Park. The blast was witnessed by hockey star Wayne Gretzky of the defending Stanley Cup champion Edmonton Oilers, who asked a *Detroit Free Press* reporter, "Holy cow! Does he do that often?" And Oiler teammate Kevin Lowe asked: "Can he skate? He's big enough to play defense."

As a boy, Gibson was greatly encouraged by his father, Bob Gibson, a former tax auditor who later became a math teacher. The elder Gibson spent lunch hours at home so he could throw footballs and baseballs to his son, and encouraged the boy to shoot baskets in the winter. "He drilled me," Gibson told the *New York Times*. "When I woke up, he had a good breakfast on the table. When I came home from school, he was waiting to play basketball. When I was down the road, he'd call me: 'Time to play catch.' I didn't always

like it, but I did it. I suppose he wanted me to do the things he didn't have a chance to do."

In an interview with the *Detroit Free Press*, Bob Gibson said of his son: "We played a lot of catch. And I'd hit him ground balls and fly balls. I hung up a baseball on the old clothesline post and I hung up an old tire for him to throw through, ideas I got from baseball coaching clinics. I probably made him play ball at times when he probably wouldn't have wanted to. I felt it kept him active and kept him out of trouble."

Of the negative publicity his son had received, Bob Gibson said: "It used to bother us. Every once in a while, we hear negative comments from people. The things about signing autographs bothers me. I don't know if Kirk always handled it well. Sometimes he may get a little gruff. I remember when he used to climb that wall in Lakeland [the Tigers Florida training camp] to avoid people. But you have to understand what it's like for him. We have 300 letters for him here right now in the house, baseball cards with stamped, self-addressed return envelopes, from all over the country, all over the world, really. His mother really puts the thumb on him and sits on him and makes him do it. His mother made him behave more than I did as far as his morals and character. I don't know how they are now, but I know she keeps on him. Basically, he's pretty good."

Gibson is the youngest of three children and the only boy. His sister Jocelyn is six years older than he; his sister Christine is five years older. In an interview with *Sports Illustrated,* Gibson said "My parents never made me work. When I grew up, all we did was screw around with motorcycles and water skiing. I had it pretty easy."

Gibson's parents later were divorced. His mother, a teacher at a suburban Detroit high school, said in a television interview on Detroit's WJBK-TV that she gets nervous and excited at ball games. "Maybe that's where Kirk gets it from," she said of her son's obvious nervous tension. "He tends to get violent about throwing his bat and his helmet. . . . I think he's grown up a lot. . . . He's a lot of fun."

Gibson also discussed his maturation in an interview with *Monthly Detroit.* "Before, I lived day to day like a party and I was comfortable going out and getting drunk every night, being in the bars, the social scene," he said, "I never cared about my family. I never cared about a relationship with any chick. Chasing women was just a big game to me. Now, if I go out, I go out with my lady to dinner with a bottle of wine." The lady of whom he spoke is JoAnn Sklarski, a former dancer, with whom Gibson lives and who Gibson plans to marry after the 1985 season. The wedding is to be a double wedding involving Dave (Rozie) Rozema, Gibson's friend and ex-teammate, who is engaged to marry Sandy Sklarski, JoAnn Sklarski's sister.

A friend of Gibson, Detroit auto dealer Joe Ricci, told *Sports Illustrated:* "Kirk has grown up a lot in the past two years. And JoAnn has had a lot to do with it. When they started hanging out together, he wouldn't let you go home until it was five o'clock in the morning. I think much of the problem was that he and Rozie both lived on the east side of town, in

Grosse Pointe. Grosse Pointe is older money. It's tradition. Anything they did seemed to contrast with that."

Gibson also credits much of his new attitude to training he received at the Pacific Institute in Seattle, Washington, where—among other things—he learned to practice positive thinking. "You create a picture of what you want to happen in your creative subconscious," he told Marney Rich of *Monthly Detroit*. "And you make an affirmation. Like: 'I'm going to hit a home run.' And you see yourself doing it. . . . What you're doing is changing your state of mind. . . . In '83 I thought I was a piece of crap. I had a bad picture then. I was out of my comfort zone. So, one of my affirmations for then was: The negative attitudes and opinions of people don't affect me." Tiger manager Sparky Anderson agrees that today's Kirk Gibson is far removed from the 1983 version as a result of this change in attitude: "He let a lot of outside people cause him animosity," Anderson commented to Rich. "He no longer lets people crucify him or crucify himself." Summarizes one of Gibson's friends: "The changes have been fabulous. . . . In the span of one year he went from goat to hero. He's gone both ends of the spectrum."

AVOCATIONAL INTERESTS: Hunting, fishing, boating.

SOURCES:

BOOKS

Anderson, Sparky, *Bless You Boys: Diary of the Detroit Tigers' 1984 Season,* Contemporary Books, 1984.

PERIODICALS

Detroit Free Press, August 8, 1978, September 3, 1982, December 16, 1982, April 10, 1983, June 15, 1983, October 17, 1984, May 13, 1985.
Monthly Detroit, April, 1985.
New York Times, October 5, 1981, March 28, 1982, October 15, 1984.
People, December 28, 1981.
Sports Illustrated, March 24, 1980, August 31, 1981, December 10, 1984, March 4, 1985.
Time, October 8, 1984.

—Sidelights by Joe LaPointe

Dwight Gooden

1964-

PERSONAL: Full name, Dwight Eugene Gooden; born November 16, 1964, in Tampa, Fla.; son of Dan (a chemical plant laborer) and Ella Mae (a nursing home aide) Gooden. *Education:* Attended high school in Tampa, Fla.

ADDRESSES: Home—Tampa, Fla.

OCCUPATION: Professional Baseball Player.

CAREER: Selected as a pitcher by the New York Mets in the first round of the 1982 free-agent draft; played for the minor league teams in the Mets' farm system, including Lynchburg of the Carolina League, where he was named Pitcher of the Year for 1983; began major league career with New York Mets, 1984—.

SIDELIGHTS: In his first season playing major league baseball, pitcher Dwight Gooden of the New York Mets set more records and won more acclaim than most pitchers do in their entire careers. Named National League Rookie of the Year for 1984, Gooden made a spectacular debut in the majors with a won-lost record of 17-9 in thirty-one starts and an earned-run average of 2.60. He pitched three shutouts, including a one-hitter against the division-winning Chicago Cubs, and was the first Met to pitch consecutive shutouts since Pat Zachry in 1980. Gooden accomplished all this when he was only nineteen years old—the youngest player in the National League.

Perhaps most outstanding was Gooden's strikeout record. Dubbed "Dr. K" by Mets fans, who hang red "K" signs over the outfield railing whenever Gooden gets a strikeout (a K is used by baseball scorekeepers to indicate a strikeout), Gooden led the majors in 1984 by striking out 276 batters. That record far exceeded the previous all-time rookie strikeout record of 245 set in 1955 by Herb Score of the Cleveland Indians. Gooden's strikeouts were earned in just 218 innings pitched, which made his ratio of strikeouts per nine innings pitched a phenomenal 11.39. He gave up only 73 walks with a strikeout/walk ratio of 3.78 to 1. The young right-hander also set a league record in September, 1984, by striking out 32 batters in consecutive games—16 against the Pittsburgh Pirates and 16 against the Philadelphia Phillies. And in neither game did he give up a walk. "You really can't pitch any better than that," Mets pitching coach Mel Stottlemyre told *Sports Illustrated.* "One thing that was clear by the end of the year was that teams weren't able to handle his pitches any better the second or third time they saw him than they were the first time. He kept getting better and better and better."

Just two years before winning Rookie of the Year honors, Gooden was a high school senior in Tampa, Florida. He was the Mets' first-round selection in the June, 1982, amateur draft after his outstanding last season at Hillsborough High

UPI/Bettmann Newsphotos

School. In 1983, the pitcher's record was 19-4 in the Mets' Class A farm team in Lynchburg, Virginia. After playing in only 40 games in two seasons in the minor leagues, Gooden expected to start the 1984 season with the Mets' Triple-A club in Tidewater, Virginia. Days before the season began, however, Mets manager Dave Johnson informed him that he would be in the Mets' four-man starting rotation at the start of the season.

What impressed observers immediately was the poise and control Gooden exhibited game after game. Even his facial expression remained consistently impassive whether he won or lost a game. As Stottlemyre commented in the *New York Times:* "The thing about Dwight is his poise. He's not going to beat himself. Other young pitchers panic or lose control in tight situations. He'll never do that. Man on third, no out, he usually makes the big pitches. That's a very unusual trait."

Gooden learned control the hard way, he told the *New York Times.* "I used to always get mad and always ended up making a fool of myself. When I was 14, I felt I was supposed to get everybody out. I got hit hard once, and lost my temper. I banged my hand up against something and hurt it, which messed me up even more. That's when I learned about control."

Gooden's dazzling fastball has been clocked at 93 m.p.h., his curveball has been described as "virtually unhittable" by teammate Rusty Staub, and Gooden, unlike many other pitchers, can throw the ball inside to great advantage. He has been compared to such pitching greats as Tom Seaver, Jim Palmer, and Steve Carlton. After facing Gooden for the first time in spring training, Seaver told *Sports Illustrated:* "What impressed me about him were his mechanics and control. I wouldn't mind having his curveball either."

In the midst of Gooden's first season, strikeout pitcher Nolan Ryan of the Houston Astros offered this assessment to the *New York Times:* "At 19, Dwight Gooden is much farther advanced than I was at that age, or Seaver or Carlton. He has control and command of his pitches, and he gets his curveball over. And you won't find a strikeout pitcher who doesn't have a good curveball to complement his fastball." The young right-hander "is so far advanced," Ryan continued, "there's no advice I could give him. The only thing I see in him is that he throws his fastball high, and the hitters chase it. But if you pitch up and make a mistake, you can get hurt. I'm not saying he can't survive up there. But the hitters adjust."

Gooden expressed surprise that major league hitters struck out so easily on his fastballs. As he told E.M. Swift of *Sports Illustrated,* "They kept telling me they'd lay off that pitch in the big leagues. But they didn't. Power hitters like that high pitch. It looks real good to them up there where they can see it. They like it, but they can't catch up to it." Perhaps the only thing that Gooden has consistent trouble with is holding runners on base. In 1984, for example, 47 of 50 runners stole bases while he was on the mound.

The 6-foot 4-inch, 190-pound pitcher combines physical grace with nearly flawless technique. Kinetics specialist Bob Toski was awestruck the first time he watched Gooden pitch, he commented to the *New York Times.* "That kid," Toski exclaimed, "has perfect synchronization of his body action when he pitches. Not just good—perfect. I couldn't take my eyes off him. He has perfect balance with his feet, legs, hips, shoulders, arm and head. He's so smooth, he doesn't even look like he's throwing as hard as he is." That Gooden is well-versed in the technical aspects of his craft was attested to by Johnson, who managed Gooden his first year in the minors. Johnson told the *New York Times:* "One day I asked him: 'How do you throw your fastball?' He said: 'I hold the ball across the seams when I want it to rise, and along the seams when I want it to sink or break.' He was 17 then. Most guys that age don't even know how to grip the

Dwight Gooden in action against the Los Angeles Dodgers, August 28, 1984. He struck out twelve batters in the game, which the Mets won 5-1. AP/Wide World Photos.

ball. But here he was, going into a 15-minute lecture on the different ways he throws his hard one."

Among the many highlights of Gooden's rookie year was being chosen to play in the 1984 All-Star Game with three of his Mets teammates, Darryl Strawberry, Keith Hernandez, and Jesse Orosco. Gooden was the youngest player ever chosen to play in the All-Star Game. When Gooden entered the game in the fifth inning the National League was ahead 2-1. As Gooden described the experience in *Playboy*, he walked out to the pitcher's mound telling himself that it was just like any other game, and all he had to do was throw strikes. "But," he related, "it wasn't just like any other game. In a regular game, I try to pace myself, but in the All-Star Game, with just two innings to pitch, I wanted to air it out and throw every pitch with everything I had. I wasn't thinking strikeouts, but I wanted to throw strikes, and I didn't want to give up any runs and lose the lead, and I didn't want to do anything like throw a wild pitch all the way to the backstop."

The first pitch he threw to Detroit Tiger catcher Lance Parrish was a fastball that Parrish took for a strike. Next Parrish fouled off a fastball to make the count 2-2. Then, Gooden commented in *Playboy*, "I decided to try to get him right there. I threw the fastball high, and he went for it and missed. I had a strikeout." Gooden used the same formula— fastballs, curveballs, and fastballs—to strike out the next two batters, Chet Lemon of the Tigers and Alvin Davis of the Seattle Mariners. By the end of Gooden's two-inning turn, he had given up only one hit and no runs. Gooden described his reception in *Playboy:* "When I walked off the mound, the crowd was standing and cheering, and it was like I was walking on air. Everybody in the dugout shook my hand and gave high fives. These were some of the best players in the game, congratulating me."

Because Gooden seems to have been born to play baseball, it's not surprising that his involvement with the sport started when he was just a toddler. Gooden's father, Dan Gooden, was formerly the coach of the Tampa Dodgers, a local semi-pro team. He introduced his son to baseball before he could even throw a ball: Dodger players would toss the ball to the three-year-old and he would roll it back. By the time the youngster started playing on teams, he was so much better than the other boys that he almost quit playing in frustration. He joined his first little league team at the age of ten as an outfielder but soon was moved to third base to take advantage of his strong arm. Gooden began pitching at the age of twelve and by fifteen was seriously considering a professional career.

Gooden was strongly encouraged by his mother Ella Mae. She told Swift: "That's all he cared to talk about, his baseball. The day he turned 17, I says to him, 'This the year for you to decide what you want to be. You can be a drug addict; you can be a drunk; you can be a nice young man and stay in school; you can be a baseball player. You decide.' He says, 'I know that.' A little later he tells me he wants to get a job at the Wendy's and what did I think. I tell him, 'you need money, you ask for it. Don't steal. But you got no time for a job. You got to play ball.' "

Unlike many other sports stars Gooden has not let success go to his head. He used part of his $40,000 rookie salary to buy a house for his parents in Tampa. He still plays catch with the neighborhood kids when he's back home, and he recalled for the *New York Times* how his high school teammates turned out to cheer him in the majors. "It was kind of unbelievable. I threw batting practice to them, and they're coming to see me throw against major league hitters. It was amazing to them. . . . I played with these guys, and now they're coming to watch me. It's something to think about."

Despite his rapid rise to stardom, Gooden is determined not to rush himself. He knows that it takes more than strikeouts to sustain a pitching career. As he told the *New York Times:* "Right now I'm just concentrating on learning the hitters. I'm not a great pitcher yet. I haven't proven myself." Manager Johnson has total confidence that Gooden will prove himself. "Truthfully," he commented to the *New York Times,* "I have run out of adjectives to describe Dwight. You pick a word, and it applies. He is just going to keep getting better and better as the years go by."

SOURCES:

BOOKS

Gooden, Dwight and Richard Woodley, *Rookie: The Story of My First Year With the Major Leagues,* Doubleday, 1985.

PERIODICALS

New York Times, February 20, 1984, April 20, 1984, May 3, 1984, May 7, 1984, June 18, 1984, July 6, 1984, July 15, 1984, July 16, 1984, July 18, 1984, August 7, 1984, September 9, 1984, November 20, 1984.
Playboy, May, 1985.
Sports Illustrated, April 15, 1985.
Time, September 24, 1984.

—Sidelights by Barbara Welch Skaggs

Mikhail Gorbachev

1931-

PERSONAL: Full name, Mikhail Sergeevich Gorbachev; born March 2, 1931, in Privolnoye, Stavropol, U.S.S.R.; married Raisa Maksimovna. *Education:* Moscow State University, law degree, 1955; Stavropol Agricultural Institute, graduate, 1967.

ADDRESSES: Central Committee, Communist Party of the Soviet Union, Kremlin, Moscow, U.S.S.R.

OCCUPATION: Soviet politician.

CAREER: Agricultural worker in Stavropol Krai, U.S.S.R., 1946-50; Stavropol City Committee, Komsomol (Young Communist League), member, beginning 1956; Stavropol City Committee, Communist Party of the Soviet Union, first secretary, 1956-58, 1966-68, second secretary, 1968-70; Stavropol Krai Committee, Komsomol, second secretary and first secretary, 1958-62, first secretary, 1970-78; deputy to U.S.S.R. Supreme Soviet, beginning 1970; Central Committee, Communist Party of the Soviet Union, member, 1971—, secretary for agriculture, beginning 1978, general secretary, 1985—. Candidate member of Politburo, 1979, full member, 1980—; chairman of Foreign Affairs Committee of U.S.S.R., beginning 1984.

SIDELIGHTS: On March 11, 1985, Mikhail Sergeevich Gorbachev became one of the most powerful men on earth when his selection as general secretary of the Communist Party of the Soviet Union placed him in command of one of the two great superpowers. He leads a nation of 273 million people whose land area covers more than one-seventh of the globe. The armed forces of the Union of Soviet Socialist Republics exceed in size and weaponry that of any other single nation and are matched only by the alliance of the United States and Western Europe. His nation, along with the United States, has fielded missiles and bombers armed with nuclear weapons sufficient to destroy civilization on much of the globe. Literally, the future of human civilization rests in part with the actions of Mikhail Gorbachev.

As general secretary, Gorbachev will be the dominant figure of the Communist Party's Politburo (Political Bureau), a self-perpetuating body of ten to fourteen men who hold supreme power in the Soviet state. Although the position of general secretary is no longer the absolute personal dictatorship it was under Joseph Stalin, when Stalin's whim had the force of law, Gorbachev's personal power will be enormous. He and his Politburo colleagues are not subject to free elections, and they control all of the major institutions of Soviet society: the armed forces, the police, the media, the schools, and the bureaucracy of the state-controlled economic system. Gorbachev's personal discretion far exceeds that available to any Western leader.

Gorbachev was nearly unknown to the West until 1982. Then, at the time of the death of long-time Soviet leader Leonid Brezhnev at age seventy-six, Gorbachev was rumored to be a possible candidate for the top position in the Soviet government. Gorbachev, then fifty-one, was the youngest member of the Politburo. The fact that he was even a possibility for general secretary meant that the long anticipated transfer of power to a younger generation of Soviet leaders might be underway. But the job went to Yuri Andropov, the sixty-eight-year-old head of the KGB, the Soviet secret police. Although chronology made Andropov one of the older generation of Soviet leaders, in the early months of his reign he called for internal Communist renewal. The renewal shook up Soviet society by cracking down on corruption, by replacing long-entrenched Communist Party and government officials, by ordering increased social discipline through a drive against worker absenteeism and inefficiency, and by expanding the power of the KGB. Gorbachev emerged in this period as Andropov's chief lieutenant and supervised implementation of Andropov's reforms. Andropov's renewal program slowed, however, when his health deteriorated. He died fifteen months after taking office.

After Andropov's death, Gorbachev was considered one of the major contenders for the succession. The Politburo, however, chose Konstantin Chernenko. Chernenko, at age seventy-two, had been close to Brezhnev and did not share the desire of Andropov and Gorbachev for an attack on the ossification of Soviet society that had developed in the latter years of Brezhnev's rule. By selecting Chernenko, the Politburo slowed the transition to a younger leadership that Andropov had begun. Nonetheless, Chernenko's age and his poor health suggested that his tenure would be relatively short; Moscow rumors held that Gorbachev was the heir apparent.

After Chernenko's selection, Gorbachev undertook an official visit to Great Britain. His career in Soviet politics had been almost entirely concerned with domestic matters. This tour served both to introduce Gorbachev to the West and to demonstrate to Gorbachev's Politburo colleagues that he could perform well on the international stage. And, indeed, his performance was superb. The West had grown used to Soviet leaders who were extremely old and often in poor health, intellectually unimpressive, and harsh or even crude in manner and speech. Gorbachev, however, was middle-aged, healthy, intelligent, and charming. Even as harsh a critic of the Soviet Union as Prime Minister Margaret Thatcher of Great Britain found Gorbachev to be a reasonable man. "I like Mr. Gobachev," said Thatcher. "We can do business together."

Gorbachev and his wife, Raisa Maksimovna, at age fifty-one, were also well dressed in the Western manner (unusual among Soviet officials) and were dubbed the "Gucci Comrades" by some Western media. Raisa Maksimovna's role in her husband's tour was also a surprise as wives of high Soviet officials usually avoid media coverage. (The Western press was unsure if Yuri Andropov's wife was even still alive before she attended her husband's funeral.) Mrs. Gorbachev, however, took a prominent role in the tour, proved to be an intelligent conversationalist (she studied philosophy at Moscow State University), and showed herself to be both photogenic and charming.

That Gorbachev was the chosen successor became clear immediately after Chernenko died on March 10, 1985. The Politburo met and announced Gorbachev's selection as General Secretary the next day. Within his first months in office, Gorbachev won full Politburo membership for three close allies. These three appointments to a body which never has more than fourteen voting members gives Gorbachev a solid majority in the Politburo and very likely assures him a long tenure.

Gorbachev was too young to participate in World War II, and that alone makes him unusual among Soviet leaders. Before Gorbachev, virtually all high Soviet officials were of a generation that came to maturity under Joseph Stalin and fought World War II, experiences that produced tough and often brutal survivors. This generation also rebuilt the Soviet Union after World War II, established its domination over Eastern Europe, and raised it to superpower status. The same generation, however, also institutionalized itself into a permanent ruling class. Communist Party officials gained virtual lifetime tenure in office, and the highest levels of the Party and the government, known as the *nomenklatura,* obtained for themselves enormous privileges not available to other Soviet citizens. These privileges included higher salaries, access to special high-quality health care, the use of state goods and workers to build or refurbish a private home and a "dacha" (a cottage in the country), access to special high-quality consumer goods at low prices, admittance to elite vacation resorts, and preferential access to elite schools and colleges for their children.

During Brezhnev's eighteen-year rule, the bureaucratization of Soviet life produced a society that was increasingly resistant to innovation. Soviet economic growth slowed significantly, and Soviet technology and science continued to lag well behind that of the United States, Japan, and Western Europe; in literature and the arts, life in the Soviet Union stifled creativity. Promotion in the upper levels of Soviet society often came through cronyism, and in some areas corruption flourished as Soviet citizens sought short-cuts through the gargantuan governmental bureaucracy.

Soviet leaders have been aware of the negative aspects of Soviet life and have attempted reforms on a number of occasions. These reform campaigns, however, were either blocked or frustrated by Communist cadre resistant to change. In the early 1960s, Nikita Khrushchev called for more rapid turnover in Party leadership. Entrenched Party cadre resented Khrushchev's plans, and, when he persisted, the Politburo deposed Khrushchev from power. Initially, Khrushchev was replaced by a dual leadership of Aleksei Kosygin and Leonid Brezhnev. In the mid-1960's Kosygin attempted to partially dismantle central economic controls. His reforms were also stifled by the bureaucracy, and he was pushed out of the leadership by Brezhnev.

Under Brezhnev, "continuity of cadre," meaning support for the tenure and privileges of the *nomenklatura,* became Soviet policy. Brezhnev recognized, however, the growing inefficiencies of the Soviet economy. On several occasions in the 1970s reform programs to partially decentralize the economy were announced, although in practice little change was noticeable. Gorbachev, in fact, won his promotion to the inner circle of the Soviet Government when he was placed in charge of implementing Brezhnev's program to decentralize agriculture. The program called for shifting control of agricultural planning from Moscow authorities to regional planners and for offering farm workers financial incentives for increased production. The results of this reform program were, however, unclear. In several years grain production fell drastically, a drop Soviet authorities attributed to poor weather. Finally, the Soviet Union stopped publishing crop production figures.

In his first months as general secretary Gorbachev's style of leadership proved to be a marked contrast to other recent Soviet leaders. He has appeared frequently on Soviet television visiting and talking with ordinary citizens and has demonstrated that he is an eloquent speaker, even without a prepared text. His wife has also taken an unprecedented high profile in Soviet media. In terms of substantive actions, Gorbachev has fired, retired, or demoted a number of officials in the Communist Party and in the government. Among those dismissed were two government ministers and nearly a dozen regional Party heads. He is attacking corruption through a reassertion of state police power, harsher and more frequent punishment for violation of economic or social discipline, and expanded KGB surveillance of domestic Soviet life. Thus far, Gorbachev has not made any significant changes in Soviet foreign policy. Nor have there been hints that Gorbachev has any desire to relax the Communist Party's monopolistic control over political and intellectual life or its policy of harsh suppression of dissidents.

Western media sometimes describe Gorbachev as a "reformer." It is an accurate term if it is understood strictly within the context of the Soviet system, a system which is hostile to democratic liberties and human rights in the Western sense. In the late 1950s Khrushchev launched a program of "de-Stalinization" to eliminate the brutal elements of Soviet life that had become institutionalized under Joseph Stalin. The KGB, the central instrument of Stalin's terror, was subordinated to other organs of Soviet government and Lavrenty Beria, Stalin's KGB chief, was executed for his bloody crimes. Other unrepentant aides of Stalin, such as Vyacheslav Molotov, were stripped of Communist Party membership and publicly condemned. For a few years a limited measure of artistic and intellectual freedom was allowed, and dissident writers such as Aleksandr Solzhenitsyn were able to publish openly.

Khrushchev began to cut back on the limited freedoms he had allowed even before his fall, and after he was removed from office a steady "re-Stalinization" took place. The KGB returned to the inner circle of Soviet power with the selection in 1982 of its head, Yuri Andropov, as general secretary of the Communist Party. Gorbachev was one of Andropov's proteges, and one of his first acts on becoming general secretary was to raise the man Andropov appointed to head the KGB to full membership in the Politburo. (By contrast, the head of the Soviet armed forces is only a "candidate" or nonvoting member of the Politburo). Stalin himself has been partially rehabilitated in Soviet history books and old unreconstructed Stalinists, such as Molotov, have been restored to Party membership. KGB harassment of intellectual, religious, and political dissenters has intensified. (Solzhenitsyn, for example, was exiled.) Further, harsh punishments are being imposed on members of non-Russian ethnic groups who resisted "Russification," and Stalin's anti-Semitism has been revived in the form of a campaign against "Zionism." There has not, however, been any use of Stalin's practice of mass terror.

Gorbachev's major concern since taking office has been the stagnation of the Soviet economy. In June, 1985, the Western press reported that Gorbachev had rejected the proposed five-year economic plan drafted by incumbent Soviet ministers. In a speech to the Central Committee, Gorbachev criticized several long-entrenched economic planners and other high economic officials associated with the Brezhnev generation. He called for revisions of the economic plan to provide for more emphasis on the quality of products, equipping plants with more modern machinery, and greater investment in research and development. Such open criticism of incumbent officials by a General Secretary is highly unusual in the Soviet Union. The *Wall Street Journal* quoted one Western expert on the Soviet economy who felt that the speech showed that Gorbachev "continues to portray the image of the new broom who comes in and really shakes thing up, a useful and dynamic person who is going to change things."

Gorbachev is reported to be sympathetic to the economic reforms suggested by the economic institute in Novosibirsk. This Soviet think-tank calls for decreased bureaucratic control of state enterprises and more flexibility for managers of these plants. In an interview with the *Wall Street Journal,* a spokesman for the institute asserted that the central planning agencies in Moscow "follow the work of enterprises too closely, and sometimes this undermines the initiative of the enterprise." In the area of agriculture, the *Washington Post* reported that Gorbachev had ordered the distribution of small plots of land to a million peasants for their private use in hopes of improving food production. Earlier, the *Washington Post* also reported that Gorbachev had asked for information on Lenin's New Economic Policy, a program in the early 1920s that allowed limited private enterprise within the Soviet economy.

Nonetheless, the same *Wall Street Journal* story citing the Soviet advocate of decentralization also quoted a spokesman for the Soviet economic planning agency, Gosplan. The Gosplan spokesman said that Gorbachev's innovations, while allowing greater flexibility and use of financial incentives to reward efficient workers and managers, will not threaten central control of the economy. Nor, it was emphasized, would Soviet economic reforms use a market mechanism to set prices, as has been done by the Communist government in Hungary. Gorbachev's speeches, although sharp in criticism of individuals, have been vague about any changes in the system of central economic control.

Gorbachev is, himself, a product of the system he wishes to revitalize. He was born in 1931 to a peasant family in Privolnoye, a village in the Stavropol territory, a farming region north of the Caucasus mountains. He graduated from law school at the Moscow State University in 1955 but never practiced law. He was admitted to the Communist Party in 1952 and served as Komsomol (Young Communist League) organizer at law school; his first professional post after graduation was as first secretary (executive head) of the Stavropol City Komsomol. He did well as a professional Party "apparatchik" and in 1958 became first secretary of the Stavropol Krai (territory) Komsomol. Then he moved further up into the Party hierarchy when he became first secretary of the Stavropol City Communist Party Committee. In 1970, he became the first secretary of the Stavropol Krai Communist Party Committee. Arkady Shevchenko, the highest ranking Soviet official ever to defect, noted in his book *Breaking with Moscow,* that Gorbachev had "earned a reputation as an energetic regional Party leader and manager . . . . He was also known as a reasonable man, with less arrogance than most professional Party apparatchiki." Shevchenko, who had met Gorbachev, described him personally as "intelligent, well educated, and well mannered."

The leadership of the Party organization in Stavropol Krai was an important post, and also a fortunate one for Gorbachev. The Stavropol region is a popular recreation area, and many high Soviet officials vacation there at elite resorts. Gorbachev, as the head of the local Communist Party, played host to these officials. Furthermore, Stavropol was the home region of Mikhail Suslov, a long-time member of the Politburo, a rigid Marxist-Leninist ideologue, and one of the leaders of the coup that forced Khrushchev from power. Suslov's patronage and Gorbachev's intimacy with many Moscow officials allowed Gorbachev to gain membership on the Central Committee of the Communist Party in 1971.

It is evidence of Gorbachev's conscienciousness that after he became Stavropol Communist Party chief that he undertook the study of agricultural issues because of the importance of farming in the local economy; in 1967 he earned a degree from the Stavropol Agricultural Institute. When the post of agricultural secretary of the Central Committee became vacant in 1978, Gorbachev was available to assume the post and move to Moscow. His work as agricultural secretary and the political allies he had developed won him full membership in the all-powerful Politburo in 1980.

Gorbachev is, then, a professional Communist functionary. His career is based upon the Communist Party's domination of the Soviet state and its monopoly of political, economic, and social power. It is unlikely that he has any desire to fundamentally change that system. What he appears to want to do, however, is to revitalize it by eliminating its corrupt and ossified elements, to bring in fresh and younger leaders, and to reduce the drag of bureaucracy on economic growth.

SOURCES:

BOOKS

Shevchenko, Arkady N., *Breaking with Moscow,* Knopf, 1985.

PERIODICALS

Detroit Free Press, March 4, 1985, March 12, 1985, March 13, 1985, March 17, 1985.
Foreign Affairs, spring, 1985.
Newsweek, June 3, 1985.
New York Times Biographical Service, March, 1985.
Time, March 25, 1985.
Wall Street Journal, May 23, 1985, June 12, 1985.
Washington Post, June 4, 1985.

—Sidelights by John E. Haynes

Chester Gould

1900-1985

OBITUARY NOTICE: Born November 20, 1900, in Pawnee, Okla.; died of congestive heart failure following a long illness, May 11, 1985, in Woodstock, Ill. Cartoonist. The creator of "Dick Tracy," Chester Gould was considered a pioneer in the field of the cartoon comic strip. Gould demonstrated his talent and interest long before the debut of his most famous character. At the age of twelve he won his first cartoon contest; while in high school he enrolled in a cartoon-art correspondence course. Gould was a cartoonist for the *Tulsa Democrat* and the *Oklahoma City Daily Oklahoman* before moving to Chicago to attend Northwestern University. Upon graduation in 1923, he joined the staff of the *Chicago American*, where he introduced "Fillum Fables," a comic strip satirizing Hollywood movies of the day. In the spring of 1931 he created the hawk-nosed, square-jawed detective that was to become his trademark. Gould drew his character with the picture of a young, modern Sherlock Holmes in mind. He sold the series, which he had titled "Plainclothes Tracy," to the *Chicago Tribune-New York Daily News* Syndicate. Joseph Patterson, publisher of the *New York Daily News*, rechristened the strip "Dick Tracy," deriving the first name from the slang word for detective. "Dick Tracy" premiered on October 4, 1931, in the *Detroit Mirror*.

Gould's inspiration came from his, and the general public's, frustration with Prohibition-era gangsters and crime. Gould wanted to create "a symbol of law and order, who could 'dish it out' to the underworld exactly as they dished it out—only better,"he explained in *Comics and Their Creators*. "An individual who could toss the hot iron right back at them along with a smack on the jaw thrown in for good measure." Yet "Dick Tracy" proved to be more than a vent for public frustration. It became the first successful, present-day adventure comic strip. Unlike his predecessors, Gould treated topical issues and set his stories in modern locales; he was the first cartoonist to depict—sometimes graphically—urban violence. Moreover, the series introduced the average reader to the concepts of two-way wrist radios, closed-circuit television, space shuttles, and heart transplants.

The strip's most popular feature, however, has been its panoply of characters, from the moody but devoted Tess Trueheart and the dull but faithful Pat Patton to such villains as B-B Eyes, Mumbles, Flattop, and Peaches de Cream. Gould received numerous awards and citations for "Dick Tracy," including the National Cartoonists Society's Reuben Award and the Mystery Writers of America's Edgar Award. He retired in 1977, leaving the comic strip to his proteges Dick Locher and Max Collins. "He pioneered our

AP/Wide World Photos

field," Locher told Wes Smith and Kenan Heise of the *Chicago Tribune*. "You could walk into his pictures and be part of his strip. When Gravel Gertie talked to B.O. Plenty, you could smell [him], and when he spit tobacco, you wanted to jump out of the way."

SOURCES:

BOOKS

Horn, Maurice, editor, *The World Encyclopedia of Comics*, Chelsea House, 1976.
Sheridan, Martin, *Comics and Their Creators*, Hyperion Press, 1971.

PERIODICALS

Chicago Tribune, May 12, 1985, May 13, 1985.
Newsweek, May 20, 1985.
Time, May 20, 1985.

Charity Grant

1974-

BRIEF ENTRY: Born 1974, in Iowa City, Iowa. American youth who stirred national controversy when she refused an award from a local club that bans women from its membership. Charity Grant was ten years old and in the fourth grade in 1984 when she was offered, and subsequently refused, the "good reading award" from the Coralville Noon Optimist Club, citing as her reason the organization's men-only membership policy.

This seemingly unremarkable act—the refusal by a ten-year-old of an obscure award given by a small club in Iowa—drew a surprising amount of national media attention and resulted in Grant receiving a great deal of mail, both pro and con, from around the country. A woman from West Virginia wrote to say that refusing the award was impolite and that Grant had displayed bad manners. Grant's response, according to *Ms.* writer Julie Gammack: "It's good she did that, she expressed how she felt. . . . That's her point of view." Grant also received crank calls, and some of her schoolmates teased her after the news stories started coming out. Grant says: "That's their problem. . . . They've got to be pretty insecure."

Overall, most of the response to the incident has been positive. Grant has received numerous letters from people—mostly women—praising her for her courage and for her sensitivity to discrimination. Her parents, too, have been supportive of her stand. They told Gammack that they feel this experience has made their daughter more "thoughtful" and "aware." Grant is convinced that by the time she reaches adulthood women will have attained equality. "I think that with all the women fighting for women's rights," she stated to Gammack, "discrimination will probably stop." In the future, Grant says, she intends to run for political office, "probably as a Democrat."

SOURCES:

PERIODICALS

Ms., January, 1985.

AP/Wide World Photos

Marvelous Marvin Hagler

1954-

PERSONAL: Name originally Marvin Nathaniel Hagler; legally changed in 1980; born May 23, 1954, in Newark, N.J.; son of Robert James Sims and Ida Mae Hagler; married Bertha Joann Dixon, June 21, 1980; children: Gentry, James, Celeste, Marvin, Charelle. *Education*: Dropped out of school in ninth grade. *Religion:* Baptist.

ADDRESSES: Marvelous Enterprises, Inc., P.O. Box 336, Brockton, Mass. 02403.

OCCUPATION: Professional boxer.

CAREER: Worked in a toy factory after dropping out of school at age fourteen; worked at a variety of jobs while boxing as an amateur; professional boxer, 1973—, World Boxing Association middleweight champion, 1980—.

MEMBER: World Boxing Association, U.S. Boxing Association, World Boxing Council, Kiwanis.

SIDELIGHTS: The place was a boxing ring in the parking lot of the Caesars Palace hotel and casino in Las Vegas, Nevada. The date was April 15, 1985, income tax day for most Americans and a payday in more ways than one for a bald, ambidextrous, Massachusetts-based boxer legally named Marvelous Marvin Hagler. By defeating Thomas Hearns with a third-round, technical knockout in a vicious middleweight boxing title defense that warm night at the gambling oasis in the desert, Hagler had earned not only a $5.7 million purse but also something less tangible and, perhaps to him, more precious. He'd finally earned, at the age of thirty and after fifteen years as a boxer, respect from the world of his sport, the admission of its intelligentsia that he was one of the best of his generation at his profession. In the immediate reaction after the bout, the national news media declared his victory over Hearns to be one of the most savage and exciting championship bouts of the modern era. "Without a doubt, this fight—which Hagler had predicted would be a 'war'—will be remembered, despite its brevity, as one of the great ring classics of recent years," the *Detroit Free Press* wrote. "A screaming throng of 15,128 roared from the opening bell to the finish as Hearns and Hagler traded awesome, crushing blows."

Until then, Hagler wasn't unanimously admired in the boxing world. Although a champion since 1980, he had scored an unimpressive victory over Roberto Duran on November 10, 1983, seventeen months before his bout with Hearns. Even though he had successfully defended his 160-pound, middleweight title against Duran, he did it with a fifteen-round decision, not a knockout. *Sports Illustrated* magazine had headlined its story, "Marvin Was Something Less Than Marvelous" and had said in the concluding paragraphs of its article, "The winner stepped out of the ring with $8 million and his image diminished."

AP/Wide World Photos

Before the fight with Hearns, Hagler told the *New York Times*: "I have a lot to prove. People have not been giving me the credit I deserve. Thomas Hearns has been lucky. He can make the big money, he can move to different divisions. But I can take anything Tommy Hearns can deliver. He's going to have to hit me with that ring post to knock me out. . . . This fight comes down to who can take the hardest shot, who can take the most punishment. I've been through the bumps and bruises and I don't think he has." Over the years, Hagler had been frustrated with his lack of recognition and the time he had to wait to get a title fight. According to a *People* report, Joe Frazier, the former heavyweight boxing champion, once told him that his biggest problems were "You're black, you're a southpaw and you can fight." Hagler, it seemed, was too dangerous for most talented boxers to risk fighting. "I used to think, 'What do I have to do, kill somebody to get the notoriety?,' " Hagler said in a *New York Times* interview. "It's a terrible thought, but what I learned is, you have to keep trucking, you have to keep the faith. This fight [with Hearns] is at the right time because I'm mature enough to want it, mature enough to handle it."

Although he had beaten Hearns to the canvas, Hagler had not escaped the bout without sustaining physical damage. In fewer than eight minutes of boxing, he had been hit by 94 of Hearns 166 punches. (He'd hit Hearns 96 times in 173 attempts). Moments after Hearns had been carried to his corner, Hagler stood for an interview in the center of the ring, blood streaming down his face from two cuts as his three-year-old daughter, Charelle, was handed to him. She wore a pink dress. Hagler lifted her into his arms, pointed out his wounds and said to her: "Hi, baby. See Daddy's boo-boos?" He resumed his interview with Home Box Office television by saying his future plan for the child compels him to do what he does. "I'm waiting to send her to school, to college one day," Hagler said as he kissed the baby and handed her gently back to her mother. "So I gotta keep it up. In ten years, who knows what the money will be to go to school?"

Hagler, although he has said he still wishes to pursue higher education, dropped out of high school in Brockton, Massachusetts, to pursue a career in boxing. He was born in Newark, New Jersey, the first child of Ida Mae Hagler and Robert Sims. His father left the family when Hagler was a child. Hagler also had a brother, Robbie, and four sisters, Veronica, Cheryl, Genarra and Noreen. His mother moved the family to Brockton after Newark's civil disturbances of 1967 and 1969. Hagler recalled the race riots in an interview with the *Detroit Free Press*. "It was funny," he said. "Like a free-for-all. Bunch of hatred. Lots of innocent people hurt. People walking into stores and taking things. Lot of bad feeling between black and white."

Hagler, in some stories, has been portrayed as one who did not mingle with other children. "Hagler was a fatherless loner who turned Ida Mae's back porch into a clinic for wounded birds and a coop for raising and training pigeons," *Sports Illustrated* reported. "A turtle lived on the fire escape, and to Ida Mae's dismay, Marvin even let it swim in the family tub." Hagler called the animals "Maybe the only friends I really liked. I was always by myself."

In 1970, he met his current boxing handlers, brothers Guareno (Goody) Petronelli and Pascuale (Pat) Petronelli, partners in a Brockton construction company. Goody is officially listed as the trainer, Pat as the manager. He first met the Petronelli brothers in Brockton when he was fifteen years old, and he first boxed professionally in Brockton in 1973, after winning fifty of fifty-two amateur fights. He also worked for the Petronellis, digging ditches and cutting down trees. Brockton is the hometown of former boxing champion Rocky Marciano, and the Petronellis had known him as a youth.

As a young fighter, Hagler was known as brash, and confident, and motivated, despite the small wages he earned at the time. In a *Sports Illustrated* article, Hagler told why he wanted a fight against Don Wigfall, another boxer from Brockton. The two had exchanged angry words at a party when Hagler was sixteen years old. When the men stepped outside to settle their differences, Hagler said he tried to take off his leather jacket. "Before I could get my jacket off, he'd decked me," Hagler said. "I rolled under a car, my jaw was swollen." In their official bout, three years later, at Brockton High School gymnasium, Hagler won a decision in eight rounds. "Every time I had the chance to put him out, I let

him back into the fight," Hagler said. "I whupped him, right in front of all the people who had seen him deck me that night." It was his fourth pro fight, and he earned $1000.

He lost two consecutive fights in 1976. One was to Bobby (Boogaloo) Watts, in Philadelphia. Two months later, Willie (the Worm) Monroe defeated Hagler in a ten-round decision. Hagler later defeated Monroe twice in rematches. Their third bout, on February 15, 1977, gave Hagler the confidence he would carry in later bouts. "That was the fight that made him," said Philadelphia promoter J. Russell Peltz. By his fiftieth bout, against Vito Antuofermo for the middleweight championship in 1979, he was called by his fans "the uncrowned middleweight champion of the world." Antuofermo retained his title that night on a draw, but after Antuofermo lost his title to Alan Minter, Hagler defeated Minter in London later that year for the title. Before the fight with Minter, Minter had been quoted in the British press as having said he wouldn't lose the title to a black man. Hagler bloodied Minter above both eyes, and the fight was stopped in the third round as Hagler dropped to his knees in thanks. When he defeated Minter, a shower of bottles and other debris fell on the ring. But when he arrived back home in Massachusetts, a crowd of 10,000 cheered for him at Brockton City Hall.

Hagler makes for an imposing physical figure. He is 5 feet, 9½ inches tall and about 160 pounds, and he has a 70-inch "reach." His body is lean and muscled. He has medium-brown skin and a Fu Manchu mustache. His head is shaved of hair. He has a deeply scarred right eyebrow, covered much of the time by sunglasses.

In 1982, he drove a white Cadillac Fleetwood Brougham with a license plate that said "CHAMP M.H." Instead of a horn, the car played a recording of the song "La Cucaracha." "It's good for the kids," he told the *Detroit Free Press*. Hagler has said he wants to take business courses, to be a movie star, and to appear in public-service messages on television aimed at young persons. His mother said she thought Hagler would grow up to be a social worker because "he loved little kids."

His regular training camp is in Provincetown, Massachusetts, a small town on the tip of Cape Cod. It is known for, among other things, its ocean location, its homosexual community, and its artistic sense. He prefers the traditional boxing training method of getting away from all distractions for a monastic existence before a big bout. The Petronelli brothers, who train him, call it "going to jail." "I get mean here," he told *Sports Illustrated*. "I've gotten meaner since I've become champion. They're all trying to take something from me that I've worked long and hard for, years for, and I like the feeling of being champ. There's a monster that comes out of me in the ring. I think it goes back to the days when I had nothing. It's hunger, I think that's what the monster is, and it's still there." In Brockton, at the door of his gym, a sign says "No women allowed." When he does his situps in training, his handlers play "Theme from Rocky" on a speaker system. At home, he sleeps in a bed with a blue velour bedspread and a gold headboard. He still raises homing pigeons. He trains by running five to fifteen six-minute miles each dawn in heavy electrician's boots. He has said his favorite color is red because "that's the blood color." He wears red boxing gloves. He is a left-handed boxer who

An elated Marvelous Marvin Hagler raises his arms in celebration after his victory over Thomas Hearns (left, being supported by the referee) in their world middleweight championship bout in Las Vegas, April 15, 1985. AP/Wide World Photos.

can switch his stance, a tactic that seemed to confuse Hearns in their showdown.

Hagler had entered the bout with Hearns with a career record of 60-2-2. Fifty of Hagler's victories had been achieved by knockout. He had not lost a fight since 1976, when he lost two consecutive bouts, the only two defeats of his professional career. Hearns was 40-1-0, with 30 knock-outs. They had been scheduled to fight in 1982, but the bout was canceled when Hearns announced he had an injured finger. Hagler said often afterward that Hearns, more highly publicized and better-paid at that point, had avoided Hagler because of fear. When they eventually met, the bout lasted only seven minutes and forty-nine seconds.

Although Hearns didn't fall to the floor until the third round, Hagler may have won the bout in the first, when he began to get the best of Hearns, who had broken a bone in his right hand by hitting Hagler. A computer counted that 165 punches had been thrown in the round, 82 by Hagler, 83 by Hearns. "It was a sensational opening round," *Sports Illustrated* reported. "Both fighters were rocked during the violent toe-to-toe exchanges, and midway through the round the champion's forehead over his right eye was ripped open either by a Hearns right hand or elbow. With Hagler not

bothering with defense, Hearns went for the quick kill. His gloves became a red blur as he rained punch after punch on the champion's head—and it would prove his undoing." As Emanuel Steward, Hearns's manager and trainer, said later of Hearns, "He fought twelve rounds in one."

Despite the edge Hagler held going into the third round, Hearns still had a good chance to win due to the condition of Hagler's facial cuts. In the third round, referee Richard Steele called time out and asked Dr. Donald Romeo, the chief physician of the Nevada State Athletic Commission, to examine the cut on Hagler's forehead and another under the eye. He asked Hagler if he would be able to continue. "No problem," said Hagler. "I ain't missing him, am I?" Less than a minute later, Hearns had been chased across the ring, hit with a series of punches, and had landed, eyes rolling, on his back.

By mid-1985, his actions had convinced the skeptics. Among his earlier admirers is Reg Gutteridge, author of *The Big Punchers*. In the book, Gutteridge wrote: "Marvin Hagler can box or brawl ambidextrously, a consummate pro who destroys the belief of the misinformed boxing followers that the men of the eighties cannot match the old-timers. . . . The accuracy of Hagler's hitting has not been surpassed by any champion. . . . He destroys (opponents) with a versatility that not only hurts but also humiliates."

SOURCES:

BOOKS

Gutteridge, Reg, *The Big Punchers*, Hutchinson (London), 1983.

PERIODICALS

Detroit Free Press, April 23, 1982, April 16, 1985, April 17, 1985.
Detroit News, April 16, 1985.
Newsweek, January 1, 1979.
New York, November 14, 1983.
New York Times, December 1, 1979, December 2, 1979, February 17, 1980, April 18, 1980, September 28, 1980, June 16, 1981, October 5, 1981, October 31, 1983, October 21, 1984, October 22, 1984, December 14, 1984, April 14, 1985.
People, November 14, 1983.
Sports Illustrated, April 17, 1978, October 6, 1980, January 26, 1981, June 22, 1981, October 18, 1982, November 8, 1982, February 21, 1983, June 6, 1983, November 21, 1983, November 14, 1983, April 8, 1985, April 22, 1985.
Time, November 21, 1983.

—Sidelights by Joe LaPointe

Patricia Roberts Harris

1924-1985

OBITUARY NOTICE: Born May 31, 1924, in Mattoon, Ill; died of cancer, March 23, 1985, in Washington, D.C. The daughter of a railroad-car waiter and a schoolteacher, Patricia Roberts Harris became the first black woman to serve as a U.S. ambassador and to hold a cabinet post. A graduate of Howard University and George Washington University Law School, Harris actively supported the civil rights movement, participating in sit-ins and other demonstrations while a student. From 1960 to 1961 she was a trial lawyer with the Justice Department. President Lyndon Johnson appointed her ambassador to Luxembourg in 1965, a position she held until 1967, when she returned to Howard University as a professor of law. Harris was named dean of the Law School in 1969, but she resigned that same year after a series of confrontations with students. In 1977, after seven years as a partner in a Washington law firm, Harris became secretary of Housing and Urban Development (HUD) under President Jimmy Carter, and from 1979 to 1980 she served as secretary of Health, Education, and Welfare (HEW).

Harris made an unsuccessful bid for mayor of the District of Columbia in 1982. Shortly before her death she was a professor of law at George Washington University. Harris received numerous awards and honorary degrees, including the Black Enterprise Achievement Award and LL.D.s from Tufts University, Johns Hopkins University, and American University. Frequently characterized as a diligent, shrewd, tough, and blunt-spoken administrator, Harris was credited with restoring order and direction to HUD and HEW.

AP/Wide World Photos

SOURCES:

PERIODICALS

Chicago Tribune, March 25, 1985.
Newsweek, April 1, 1985.
New York Times, March 24, 1985.
Time, April 1, 1985.

Jack Horner

1946-

PERSONAL: Full name, John R. Horner; born 1946, in Shelby, Mont.; divorced; children: Jason. *Education:* Attended University of Montana for seven years.

ADDRESSES: Office—Museum of the Rockies, Montana State University, Bozeman, Mont. 59715.

OCCUPATION: Paleontologist.

CAREER: Princeton University, Princeton, N.J., fossil preparator in museum, 1975-82; Montana State University, Museum of the Rockies, Bozeman, curator of paleontology, 1982—. *Military service:* U.S. Marine Corps; served in Vietnam.

WRITINGS: Contributor of articles to journals, including *Nature* and *Scientific American.*

SIDELIGHTS: Because of his discoveries of dinosaur nesting sites and fossilized eggs, paleontologist Jack Horner has called into question long-held scientific beliefs. Since 1978, Horner has uncovered more than four hundred fossilized dinosaur eggs and eight dinosaur nesting sites at an archeological dig in northwestern Montana. His finds suggest that dinosaurs cared for their young, a discovery that contradicts what science has believed about dinosaurs for many years. Until Horner's discovery, it was assumed that dinosaurs, like present-day reptiles, simply laid their eggs and abandoned them. To find nesting sites implies that dinosaurs had some sort of family structure and were capable of forming social groups. Horner even speculates that dinosaurs may have been warm-blooded animals. His conclusions, writes David Quammen in *Esquire,* are "a little like announcing, five hundred years ago, that the earth isn't flat after all."

A native of Montana, Horner came by his profession naturally. Since the 1850s, Montana has been the site of some of the world's most important finds of dinosaur fossils. It is ideal country for fossils. During the Cretaceous Period, Montana formed the western shore of a great sea. It was country favored by many species of dinosaur. When the sea withdrew from the area, dinosaur remains were preserved in the remaining sediments. Horner found his first dinosaur fossil—which he still has—at the age of eight, and his interest in paleontology began. In school, Horner did well in the sciences but dropped out of the University of Montana because of problems in completing his nonscience requirements. Horner explains to Steve Byers of *People* that he "hated the other stuff, which seemed to have no relevance to my life." Nonetheless, in 1975 he found a job with the Princeton University museum doing what he loves to do best—working with fossils. Each summer, Horner manages to return to Montana for independent fossil digs.

Photograph by Dan Root/Missoulian

Since 1978, Horner and fellow paleontologist Robert Makela have been uncovering fossils at a site in Montana called the Willow Creek Anticlime. This site is unique because it appears to have been a rookery—an area where many dinosaurs gathered to lay their eggs, much as some species of birds do today. Over four hundred dinosaur eggs of three different species have been found. "At this site," Horner writes in *Scientific American,* "unlike most other places where dinosaur remains have been found, most of the eggs are in the exact position where they were laid and most of the skeletons are in the position and apparent location where the animal died." Of special interest are the skeletons of juvenile dinosaurs, which show that young dinosaurs stayed near their mothers until they were able to fend for themselves. "Some form of extended parental care was administered," Horner and Makela write in an article for *Nature,* "for, if the young were confined to the nest, food must have been brought to them." This new species of parental dinosaur was named *Maiasaura peeblesorum* by Horner and Makela. *Maiasaura* means "good-mother reptile," while *peeblesorum* is in honor of the Peebles family, on whose land the dig is located.

"Throughout the whole history of fossil collection," Quammen states, "dinosaur eggs and juveniles have remained breathtakingly rare; no other nest full of hatchlings has *ever* been found." Already the discovery has necessitated changes in books about dinosaurs and in the way dinosaurs are depicted in natural history museums. Despite his lack of a college degree, Horner has become one of the country's leading paleontologists and one of three, along with John Ostrom and Robert Bakker, whose work was drastically transformed scientific beliefs about the dinosaurs.

Working now at Montana State University's Museum of the Rockies, Horner teaches and writes during the winter months and spends his summers at the fossil site with a crew of volunteers. Living in tepees and stocked with such supplies as "a rented jackhammer, short-handle picks, ice picks, delicate brushes, and 150 cases of beer," as Quammen observes, Horner's excavation team digs throughout the summer. "I couldn't be lured away from here by any amount of money or promised notoriety," Horner explains to Byers. Speaking to Quammen, Horner adds: "Dinosaurs are *really neat* animals."

SOURCES:

PERIODICALS

Esquire, December, 1984.
Nature, November 15, 1979.
New York Times, October 11, 1981.
People, August 27, 1984.
Scientific American, April, 1984.

—Sketch by Thomas Wiloch

Henry E. Kloss

1929(?)-

BRIEF ENTRY: Born c. 1929. American electronics executive and inventor. Henry E. Kloss is a major name in the home entertainment industry. He has invented several of its most important products, and he has helped to found four of its more successful companies. Among his inventions are the acoustic-suspension speaker and the large-screen projection television.

Kloss discovered his flair for enterprise while a student at the Massachusetts Institute of Technology during the early 1950s. There, he and some friends designed the first acoustic-suspension speaker, considered an audio breakthrough that popularized high fidelity sound. The invention's success prompted Kloss to drop out of school to start his own manufacturing firm, Acoustic Research. Later, Kloss and two partners formed a second concern, KLH, where Kloss redesigned his previous effort and eventually created the KLH Model Eleven, the world's first compact, portable stereo. When Kloss and his associates sold KLH, the inventor turned his attention to the growing video market. In 1967 he co-founded Advent with the goal of producing projection televisions. To finance this project, the company manufactured and sold loudspeakers. Kloss introduced his first projection television in 1973. Six years later he became founder and president of Kloss Video Corp., which manufactures one of his latest inventions, the Novatron tube and two-piece projection screen system. The Novatron system, experts agree, provides the clearest picture available in the large-screen projection television market.

AP/Wide World Photos

For the most part, Kloss credits his success to the shortsightedness of his competitors and to his own ability, as *Rolling Stone*'s Susan March points out, "[to combine] possibilities in ways no one else seems to envision." Referring to the projection television, Kloss told March that he intended to "develop a more desirable and commanding picture, something I guess that would resemble the movies. . . . The elements were there; I just brought them to bear."

SOURCES:

PERIODICALS

Fortune, June 29, 1981.
New York Times, December 25, 1982.
Rolling Stone, January 24, 1980.

John Lithgow

1945-

PERSONAL: Full name, John Arthur Lithgow; born October 19, 1945, in Rochester, N.Y.; son of Arthur (a theatrical producer) and Sarah L. (an actress) Lithgow; married Jean Taynton (a teacher), September 10, 1966 (divorced, 1976); married Mary Yeager (a history professor) 1981; children: Ian (first marriage); Phoebe, Nathan (second marriage). *Education:* Graduated magna cum laude from Harvard University, 1967; additional study at London Academy of Music and Dramatic Art, 1967-69.

ADDRESSES: Home—Los Angeles, Calif. *Agent*—Lund Agency, 6515 West Sunset, Los Angeles, Calif. 90028.

OCCUPATION: Actor on stage and in motion pictures; theatrical director.

CAREER: Made dramatic debut in 1951; acted in fifteen plays produced by Great Lakes Shakespearean Festival in Ohio, 1963-64; Royal Court Theatre, London, England, actor and director, 1967-69; director of five Broadway and Off-Broadway productions, 1968-70; actor in eleven Broadway and Off-Broadway productions, 1973-82; actor in motion pictures, including "All That Jazz" and "Rich Kids," both 1979, "Blow Out," 1981, "The World According to Garp" and "Dealing," both 1982, "Twilight Zone—The Movie," "Terms of Endearment," and "Footloose," all 1983, and "The Adventures of Buckaroo Banzai" and "2010: Odyssey Two," both 1984. Has also appeared in a variety of television shows. Performed on his own program, "Under the Gun," WBAI-Radio, New York, N.Y., 1972-73.

WRITINGS: Author of one-man show "Kaufman at Large."

AWARDS, HONORS: Tony Award from League of New York Theatres and Producers, 1973, for "The Changing Room"; Academy Award nominations for best supporting actor, from Academy of Motion Picture Arts and Sciences, 1982, for "The World According to Garp," and 1983, for "Terms of Endearment."

SIDELIGHTS: Versatility—the ability to play off-beat roles ranging from a psychopathic killer to a transexual ex-football player to a fiery country preacher—helped John Lithgow become one of Hollywood's most sought-after character actors by the mid-1980s. He attained prominence in his thirties, after years of respected work on Broadway. But even after his career took off through roles in films like "Terms of Endearment" and "The World According to Garp," more people knew Lithgow by face than by name. "I wouldn't mind being an unrecognized actor so long as people who know about acting know me," Lithgow told the *New Yorker* in 1977. "My reputation is extremely important. My face is not."

AP/Wide World Photos

Lithgow was born into an acting family. His mother, Sarah, was an accomplished thespian. His father, Arthur, headed Princeton University's McCarter Theater before moving the family to Ohio as a regional theater producer during John's infancy. John made his stage debut at age six in "Henry VI, Part Three," and throughout his childhood was regularly cast in the Shakespeare plays produced by his father. Still, Lithgow's earliest ambition was to become a graphic artist. He was awarded a scholarship to Harvard University and helped pay college expenses by selling his own woodblock Christmas cards. He also continued acting on the side and, by the time he earned a Fulbright scholarship to the London Academy of Music and Dramatic Art in 1967, his love for the stage was rekindled. While in England, he acted and directed with the Royal Shakespeare Company and the Royal Court Theatre.

Lithgow returned to the United States at age twenty-two to direct plays for his father's company. In 1971, he moved to New York City with his first wife, Jean Taynton, a teacher of emotionally disturbed children. After two years of struggling with bit parts, he landed his first big role as a British rugby player in the Broadway production of David Storey's "The Changing Room." Lithgow won a Tony

Award for his performance in the play, which included the only nude scene of his career.

Over the next eight years he drew enthusiastic reviews for his performances in respected Broadway and Off- Broadway productions such as "Comedians," "Once in a Lifetime" and "Anna Christie," in which he co-starred with actress Liv Ullmann. He also wrote and starred in "Kaufman at Large," a one-man show about playwright George S. Kaufman. Reviewing the play in the *New Yorker* in 1982, Edith Oliver criticized the way "in which the sardonic, unsentimental Kaufman is misleadingly portrayed as emotional and occasionally tender." Still, she allowed, "For all my objections, I was not bored or depressed, but only because Mr. Lithgow is an engaging fellow to watch under any circumstances."

Lithgow's film career began in the 1970s with what were considered forgettable roles in inconsequential films such as "Dealing," "Obsession," and "Rich Kids." But he drew notice for his performances as an envious stage director in "All That Jazz" in 1979 and a psychopathic killer in "Blow Out" in 1981. His big film break came in 1982 in "The World According to Garp," George Roy Hill's adaptation of John Irving's novel, in which Lithgow played Roberta Muldoon, a one-time tight end for the Philadelphia Eagles who underwent surgery to become a woman. He was nominated for an Oscar for best supporting actor for that work, but, ironically, Dustin Hoffman won the best actor Oscar the same year for his role as a female impersonator in "Tootsie."

In an article for *Mademoiselle* in 1982, Lithgow—a six-foot-four hulk of a man—wrote that playing a woman in "Garp" was the most challenging role of his career. "It's so much fun pretending to be another person," he commented. "But this was something else again. For those nine weeks [of filming] I contemplated one of life's basic mysteries: What does it really feel like to be a member of 'the other sex'? It was as if I was lurking around in disguise, inside the borders of some forbidden country—a spy behind the lines. . . . It was quite an experience: comical, secretive, sexy, and from time to time, more than a little confusing."

While promoting "Garp" on television, Lithgow said he would like to act in a movie directed by Steven Spielberg. When he returned home, he found a note from the famed director, offering him a part in the film version of "The Twilight Zone." The film—actually four separate episodes within one movie—was plagued from the start. A helicopter accident killed actor Vic Morrow and two Vietnamese children acting in the movie. Production was held up for two months, lawsuits were filed over the deaths and, when it was finally released, "Twilight Zone—The Movie" received poor reviews. "The deaths had such a devastating effect on the film," Lithgow told *People* magazine. "It never recovered from the dark shadow that ended three lives and ruined others."

Still, Lithgow won critical praise for his performance as a fear-crazed airline passenger who sees a space monster. *Newsweek*'s Jack Kroll called him "a human earthquake," and *Rolling Stone* declared him "a virtuoso of hysteria." In a self-analysis of his performance for a Warner Brothers press release, Lithgow said, "I wanted the character to be simply prostrate with fear—capable of anything—but it's not purely

theatrics. This a man who loses any semblance of rationality at 20,000 feet up in the air but who, when down on the ground, is completely normal." Later he called his work in the film "the best thing I've ever done."

Lithgow followed in 1983 with a small, but much-noticed role as Midwestern banker Sam Burns, who has an affair in "Terms of Endearment," a film that earned him his second Oscar nomination as best-supporting actor. In a diary of the making of "Terms" he wrote for *Film Comment*, Lithgow described his character as "shy, bumbling, faintly hayseed, but goodhearted and dignified. . . . I actually sobbed when I read the scene where they say goodbye and thought to myself, 'The audience will just die when they see this scene.' " Lithgow's diary further reflected on his chosen career: "Acting, for all its essential frivolity, is such emotionally intense and involving work that you cannot do it (or do it well, anyway) without thinking you're working on something great and important. This is why we're often deluded about the worth of a project, and why we go on and on about the incredible impact of some little moment or how the audience will just die when they see this scene. We have to believe in what we're doing, or doing it is worse than pointless; and once in a while, where we're lucky, we're right."

Lithgow's next film performance was the highly acclaimed supporting role in "Footloose," in which he played a fire and brimstone country preacher who thought the road to hell was paved with rock and roll records. Writing for *Film Comment*, Lithgow described "Footloose" as "a curious mixture of rock movie and torrid domestic drama—a sort of cross between 'Fame' and 'Rebel Without a Cause.' " Of his own character, Reverend Shaw Moore, Lithgow wrote: "I needed to be born again, in three short weeks, if I was to give this man some plausibility, dignity and sympathy. Otherwise, I'd end up the unsubtle black side of a black-and-white tale."

Lithgow made two film appearances in 1984, in "The Adventures of Buckaroo Banzai" and in "2010: Odyssey Two." In "Buckaroo Banzai," a science fiction/rock and roll fantasy, he played Dr. Emilio Lizardo, an eccentric Italian physicist possessed by the mind of an evil alien. For the role, he wore two sets of false teeth and three layers of clothes, and he acquired an accent by spending weeks mimicking an Italian tailor at MGM. Lithgow told the *Washington Post* that the film, which was a box office flop, was "the weirdest thing I've ever done." In "2010," a sequel to the tremendously successful 1968 film "2001: A Space Odyssey," Lithgow played an aerospace engineer. The film was a critical and financial failure, although Lithgow's performance was not panned by critics.

For all his success, Lithgow has yet to land the lead in a feature film but retains hope that he may, still. "I read a script in which I'm offered the third part and I say, 'Damn it, why don't they give me the first part? I can play the hell out of this,' " he told *Newsweek* in 1984. "And I think before too long they will." He told *People* magazine, however, that he does not expect to play a romantic figure. "My hairline is receding," he said. "So my days as a romantic lead—even though I've never had them—are behind me." But if he is not regarded as a star in the traditional Hollywood sense, Lithgow's work is nonetheless respected. *Newsweek*'s Jack

Kroll, for example, calls him "an actor's actor, like Robert Duvall, a guy who can play the hell out of any part."

In 1984, Lithgow took a break from Hollywood to co-star with Richard Dreyfuss as the punch-drunk fighter in "Requiem for a Heavyweight" at Connecticut's Long Wharf Theater. The performance was very satisfying, he told *Newsweek*. "You had the sense you were transfixing the audience and you were part of that transaction. A movie is different—I once said I don't think God ever intended actors to see themselves." He plans to return to films but says he will be more selective about his roles. "My agent warned me, 'You're going to be offered lots of things that need you more than you need them,'" he told the *Washington Post*.

In a *Newsweek* article, Lithgow explained his approach to acting: "You just do the best you can from shot to shot, and when you get to the end forget you were ever in it. Don't store up any hopes, don't go snooping around the editing room and don't go to early screenings because you're bound to be disappointed by the way you've been used. In this business you have to acknowledge the fact that you are just being used and all you can hope for is to be well used." He also told *Newsweek* what he hopes for in his future: "I want to retain my capacity for surprising people. And I want life to retain its capacity to surprise me. And I hope I don't lose too much hair." In addition, Lithgow has chosen an epitaph for himself. He told *People* that he wants his tombstone to read: "He was the best thing in it."

AVOCATIONAL INTERESTS: Cooking, collecting old furniture, playing the banjo.

SOURCES:

PERIODICALS

Film Comment, November-December, 1983.
Mademoiselle, September, 1982.
Newsweek, March 19, 1984.
New Yorker, January 21, 1977, January 11, 1982.
People, July 4, 1983.
Washington Post, February 21, 1984.

—Sidelights by Glen Macnow

Madonna

1958-

PERSONAL: Full name, Madonna Louise Ciccone; born August 16, 1958, in Bay City, Mich.; daughter of Silvio (an engineer) and Madonna Ciccone; married Sean Penn (an actor), August 16, 1985. *Education:* Attended University of Michigan for two years; studied dance in New York with the Alvin Ailey American Dance Theater and with Pearl Lang; studied voice in Paris.

ADDRESSES: Office—c/o Sire Records, 165 West 74th St., New York, N.Y. 10023.

OCCUPATION: Pop singer; actress.

CAREER: Drummer with band Breakfast Club in New York City for one year; formed and performed with a number of bands in New York City; currently solo performer and actress.

DISCOGRAPHY:

RECORD ALBUMS, PRODUCED BY SIRE RECORDS

Madonna (includes "Lucky Star," "Borderline," "Burning Up," "I Know It," "Holiday," "Think of Me," "Physical Attraction," and "Everybody"), 1983.
Like a Virgin (includes "Material Girl," "Angel," "Like a Virgin," "Over and Over," "Love Don't Live Here Anymore," "Dress You Up," "Shoo-Bee-Doo," "Pretender," and "Stay"), 1984.

OTHER

Recorded "Crazy for You," from the soundtrack of the film "Vision Quest," and "Into the Groove," from the soundtrack of the film "Desperately Seeking Susan"; has also recorded several twelve-inch discs.

SIDELIGHTS: She has made the belly button fashionable again. She has put rosaries and crucifixes back around the necks (and in the ear lobes) of teenage and pre-teenage girls. "Boy Toy," a legend she wears on her belt buckle, has become a symbol of tease and titillation. Through a tongue-in-cheek song called "Material Girl," she has made the pursuit of instant gratification something to be proud of. She's Madonna Louis Ciccone—Madonna to most people. And as a result of two albums, several rock videos, and a hit movie, she is the latest in trends, following Boy George, Michael Jackson, Prince and Cyndi Lauper in the line of succession for pop stardom.

She has become the siren and the scourge of American popular culture. Feminists particularly have charged her with setting their movement back in time by exploiting her body and espousing archaic, sex-kitten values. Fans, meanwhile, cheered her cheeky, carefree attitude that—during her spring, 1985, concert tour—manifested itself in an onstage challenge: "Do you believe in yourselves?" "She personifies what people would like to be but are afraid to be," explained her Los Angeles-based manager, Freddie

AP/Wide World Photos

DeMann, to the *Detroit Free Press.* "Everyone would like to be her, but they don't have the guts." Or, as Madonna herself told *Time* magazine, "My image to people, I think, is that I'm this brazen, aggressive young woman who has an OK voice with some pretty exciting songs, who wears what she wants to wear and says what she wants to say."

According to friends, teachers, and co-workers, that's the way Madonna has been all her life. She was born August 16, 1958, in Bay City, Michigan, to Chrysler/General Dynamics engineer Silvio "Tony" Ciccone (pronounced "Chick-onee" in Italian but Americanized to "Gi-kone") and his wife, who gave her own distinctive first name to her daughter. In all, there were six children from this union; Madonna was the third child, behind Anthony and Martin; following her were Paula, Christopher, and Melanie. On December 1, 1963—after the family had moved to Pontiac, Michigan—Madonna's mother died, and shortly thereafter, her father shocked the family by announcing he would marry their housekeeper, Joan. "It just didn't make any sense to me," Madonna told *Rolling Stone* magazine. "I'm sure I felt a lot of anger, . . . and I'm sure I took it out on my stepmother." One of her academic counselors, however, said the second marriage—which produced two more children, Jennifer and

Mario—didn't cause any unusual tension. "[Madonna] had several different roles in her family, but she seemed to take pride in being able to do them all," she told the *Detroit Free Press*.

A popular story that now follows Madonna is that the Ciccone family lived next door to rock star Bob Seger and his family. They did live in the same neighborhood in Pontiac, but the only contact friends can remember was one incident when Seger had car trouble and stopped at the Ciccone house for assistance.

The family, for its part, now tries to keep a low profile in the wake of Madonna's success. "I get so many calls on this," said her father to a *Detroit Free Press* reporter. "Basically, I'm happy for her success, but I don't want to say any more about this; it could be taken out of context, as so much has been." He did however, consent to take part in Madonna's stage show, dragging her offstage as a taped voice boomed over the speakers, ordering the star to "come home this instant."

It seems hard to find anyone from Madonna's past who's surprised at her success. Even during her early school days—at St. Frederick's in Pontiac and St. Andrews and West Junior High in Rochester, Michigan—Madonna, one teacher told the *Detroit Free Press,* "had this attitude like, 'Yeah, I'm gonna be somebody. You all just watch me.'" Agreed Carol Lintz, a French teacher at Rochester Adams High School: "She never bothered with the whole peer thing, other than, 'I'm gonna be somebody.'. . . Her . . . personality was well on its way to forming by the time she was here."

No matter what she may have dreamed for her future, Madonna kept herself in a college preparation program all through high school. She was often on the honor roll (her record is mostly A's and B's), scored well on the SAT tests, and scored in the top 10 percent on a verbal intelligence test. Counselor Nancy Ryan Mitchell's recommendation on a scholarship application to the University of Michigan described her as having an "extremely talented, dedicated, motivated, sparkling personality." Her record is also filled with extra-curricular activities, including junior-varsity cheerleading, choir, Latin club, swimming instructor at the Rochester community pool, and volunteering in Help-A-Kid, a variation of the Big Brother program. She ended up graduating early, in the middle of the 1975-76 school year.

"She spent her high school years zipping out of here," Mitchell recalled in the *Detroit Free Press*. "I didn't counsel her; she came to me and told me what she was going to do. At that time she talked mostly about dance. She knew she was good and wanted to be famous and would work hard to make it." Many teachers at Rochester Adams remember Madonna's dancing. At school dances, she would just get out on the floor and start dancing by herself. "She'd be in front of the cafeteria, just really letting it loose," said Carol Lintz. "The other kids would walk up to me and say, 'Who's Madonna dancing with?' The music started and her whole body filled with it, like she was alone with the music." Madonna was also active in starting the school's Thespian Society, a theater troupe that performed several skits and one play, "Dark of the Moon." During her tenure, she won the club's first Outstanding Senior Thespian award and also

came up with the first fund-raising idea—a pie sale. Yearbook pictures from her final year also show Madonna's shift from neat, suburban grooming to what was then considered a more natural appearance, wearing little make-up and letting her hair grow. As choir teacher Alan Lintz told a *Detroit Free Press* writer, "She had a real European kind of attitude, a real cosmopolitan flair. She dared to be different."

Some of that attitude can be traced to Madonna's out-of-school education, hours spent with private dance instructor Christopher Flynn, who ran the Christopher Ballet in Rochester until it closed in 1976. Flynn and Madonna—who started studying with him in 1972—struck up a friendship outside of class as well. The two would go for long drives or catch the latest fashions, music, and dances at local Detroit clubs. "We used to go mostly to the gay bars because the disco dancing was so good," Flynn, fifty-four, recounted in the *Detroit Free Press*. "She could very quickly attune to any atmosphere. She'd be totally relaxed and get into it, then come out and be a totally different person. . . . To me, what's so interesting is this incredible image that's up there. They see the obvious, the bare midriff, the sleaze, . . . which is fine, because that's what the image is about. I know her behind that, not a different person, but a complete person."

Both Madonna and Flynn ended up in Ann Arbor, Michigan, in the fall of 1976, Madonna to study and Flynn to teach in the University of Michigan dance department. One of her roommates was Whitley Setrakian, a dance department student who had transferred from a small college in upstate New York and was looking for someone to share a room with. "One of the first things I noticed was she really said what was on her mind," said Setrakian (now artistic director for an Ann Arbor dance troupe) to the *Detroit Free Press*. "The first day she looked at the apartment, I was really depressed and she immediately said, 'Whitley, you don't look very happy.' She just plunged into being really, really direct."

The two had much in common. Both worked at an ice cream parlor, " 'til our arms were raw," and they enjoyed reading poetry. Setrakian called Madonna "My Little Bowl of Bear Mush" after a whole-grain cereal she ate, though she could just as often be found eating large amounts of popcorn. At night, they and a third friend, Linda Alaniz, would hit Ann Arbor clubs such as the Blue Frogge and the Ruvia. "It was crazy," said Alaniz, now a photographer with Martha Swope Studio in New York. "We'd dance six hours at school, then go home and eat, then dance another four hours at night. The woman just loved to dance."

Madonna and Alaniz were in a University production called "Stations of the Cross," based on the religious ritual, and were rehearsing in a nearby church. "During one of the breaks, Madonna got up on the pulpit and started singing, 'Good golly Miss Molly, sure like to ball,'" Alaniz remembered. "The teacher just screamed at her, 'Madonna, stop that! It's sacrilegious!'" Alaniz also remembered going back to Madonna's dormitory room in Stockwall Hall—where she lived shortly before moving in with Setrakian—after finishing work at Dooley's Bar. One of the first things she would do is put her tips into a book about the New York Ballet. "Every time I'd come she'd open this book and show me how much money she had," Alaniz remembered. "She was getting ready to come to New York, getting her kitty together for the real world. It's such a change to think of Madonna worth millions of dollars when I used to buy her salad."

The millions—multi-millions actually—were still in the distant future when Madonna got off the bus in New York carrying a rag doll during the fall of 1978. She didn't have immediate plans, but she was able to get some modeling jobs (during which were taken the nude photographs that were later sold—amid much publicity—to *Penthouse* and *Playboy* magazines). And she eventually won a work-study scholarship and took classes with the Alvin Ailey American Dance Theater's third company, which *Rolling Stone* described as "a little like getting a tryout for the sub-junior-varsity team." Still, "I thought I was in a production of 'Fame,' " Madonna told *Rolling Stone*. "Everyone was Hispanic or black, and everyone wanted to be a star." She left Ailey's troupe after a few months and hooked up with Pearl Lang, who used to work with choreographer Martha Graham. But about the same time, she discovered an interest in rock and roll music through Dan Gilroy, who lived in an abandoned synagogue with his brother Ed. He taught Madonna the rudiments of guitar and drums, and before long she was singing with their group, Breakfast Club.

Before long, however, Madonna was whisked away to Paris to sing backup and dance for disco star Patrick Hernandez. The trip was a bust, and Madonna returned to New York to work once more with the Gilroys. By 1981 she was out of that group again due to internal disagreements. She eventually sought out Steve Bray, a former boyfriend from Michigan, and they began writing songs together and formed a number of bands, including the Millionaires, Modern Dance and Emmy.

The club gigs caught the attention of one music mogul who put her on salary and gave her a place on New York's Upper West Side. Madonna and Bray formed a new band—named simply Madonna—playing funkier, more danceable material. It was Mark Kamins of Danceteria, a trend-setting Manhattan club, who brought a tape of her songs to Sire Records. The record company signed her, and the marketing of Madonna began in earnest.

The original strategy, according to Michael Rosenblatt—then in charge of signing and developing new acts for Sire—was to introduce Madonna through the dance clubs. "I thought we had something special here, so I didn't want to throw out just another great album by another great new artist," Rosenblatt explained to the *Detroit Free Press*. "Instead of recording an album very fast, we did it slowly. We put out a 12-inch [one song on an album-sized disc; very popular in dance clubs], and when that worked, we put out another." The strategy for that first song, "Everybody," according to Bobby Shaw, then head of national dance promotion for Warner Bros. Records—which distributes Sire—was to "get the record played in the clubs, then cross it over from clubs to radio." And it worked; the song was a number three hit on the dance charts and was played on urban contemporary radio.

The same thing happened with the next twelve-inch discs—"Burning Up/Physical Attraction" and "Holiday"—but

Madonna still wasn't getting the kind of attention Shaw and Rosenblatt thought she deserved. "They were selling like crazy, but nobody at Warner Bros. seemed to care about it at the time," Shaw told the *Detroit Free Press*. "A lot of record companies won't push an artist until an album's out."

Once the first album, *Madonna,* came out in early 1983, it was evident that Madonna needed a high-powered manager to guide her career. She asked Rosenblatt who the best was; he told her Freddie DeMann, who at the time was busy guiding Michael Jackson's *Thriller* to history-making proportions. Something about her appealed to DeMann. As he explained to the *Detroit Free Press:* "What she has is undefinable, in my opinion. Very few of our stars have it. Michael Jackson has it, and Madonna has it." DeMann set about turning whatever it was into one of the hottest female acts of the eighties using an innovative and effective music-video coupling.

The first step was to cross Madonna over from the dance to the mass audience. In "Borderline," they had a song Shaw said "was more a pop and not as much a dance record as the others." And for "Lucky Star," according to DeMann, "we did this inexpensive performance video, and she came across so tantalizing, she just drove everybody crazy." Indeed, it was the video for the latter—which featured Madonna purring and puckering to the camera between shots of her bare belly-button—that pushed her way to the top. "I couldn't be a success without also being a sex symbol," she told *Spin* magazine. "I'm sexy. How can I avoid it?" To *People,* she said, "Bruce Springsteen was born to run. I was born to flirt."

The combination of her come-hither personality plus her above-average skills in dance and singing spurred sales of more than two million copies of her first album and made her fare for every music and popular magazine, from *People* to *Rolling Stone* to the *National Enquirer*. Her romances—most notably with producer John "Jellybean" Benitez and actor Sean Penn (to whom she is now married)—have been widely chronicled, and she was chased by photographers at parties and at restaurants.

Feminists, meanwhile, screamed that her seductive tactics were setting the image of women backwards, and other detractors wrote her off as a pre-programmed star who was more style than substance. "I think people want to see me as a little tart bimbo who sells records because I'm cute, and record companies push 'em because they know they can make a quick buck on my image," Madonna told *Record* magazine. "I try to have thick skin, but every once in a while I read something that someone says about me, and it's so slanderous and moralistic and it has nothing to do with my music. . . . The fact of the matter is that you can use your beauty and use your charm and be flirtatious, and you can get people interested in your beauty. But you cannot maintain that. In the end, talent is the only thing. My work is the only thing that's going to change any minds."

Regardless of what people thought, Madonna stormed into 1985 with twice the momentum she had the previous two years. The *Like a Virgin* album and single, which had debuted on the MTV Video Awards program a couple months earlier, shot straight into the top ten; the album eventually sold more than four million copies. DeMann, meanwhile, channeled Madonna's career towards the silver screen. He wanted her to have the lead role in "Vision Quest," but by the time he put his bid in, all that remained was the part of a nightclub singer. Good enough, he thought, and all the better, in that the film was scheduled for a fall, 1984, release, just as the *Like a Virgin* album would be coming out. Then came the title role for the film "Desperately Seeking Susan," a part DeMann said was made for Madonna: "The character Susan, that's exactly what Madonna is. There's almost no acting involved there. That's her—her personality, her lifestyle, her dress."

So the plan was set—a movie cameo in the fall, followed by an album at Christmas, then another movie in the spring and, finally, her first tour. Things went awry, however, when "Vision Quest" was postponed and became an early 1985 release, not too far in front of "Susan." In a five-month period, then, Madonna had songs on three new albums and her face in two new movies. "Suddenly, I had a lot of music to contend with," DeMann said. The danger of which, he pointed out, was fragmenting interest in the songs. "I want all our records in the top five, top ten for sure. Anything less I consider a failure."

Excess, in this case, meant success, however. "Material Girl," the second single from the *Like a Virgin* album, hit number one, as did "Crazy for You" from "Vision Quest." Both, in fact, were in the top five at the same time. The follow-up single from the album, "Angel," also glided up the charts, and a song from "Desperately Seeking Susan," entitled "Into the Groove," became all the rave at dance clubs.

Her next step was to conquer the nation's concert stages, and it barely took any effort. DeMann originally wanted the "Like a Virgin" tour to play small, three-thousand-seat halls so they'd "still leave people waiting, and that way create a hot ticket." But those small venues sold out in minutes, and one promoter told DeMann he could have sold another 36,000 tickets. So later dates of the tour were upgraded to large arenas, and Madonna sold them out with ease; indeed, she became the hot ticket for the first half of 1985, just as Michael Jackson and Prince had split ticket sales in 1984.

DeMann says that after all the hype and hoopla, Madonna's future remains bright. And few disagree with him. Even the publication of the nude photographs in the September, 1985, issues of *Penthouse* and *Playboy* failed to diminish her popularity as some early observers suspected it might. Madonna was honest about the photos right from the beginning, maintaining that she saw no reason to be ashamed of them, and her career appears not to have suffered in the slightest from the controversy. DeMann has already planned another movie for the spring of 1986 with an album to follow in the summer. He was even considering another tour for late 1985. Said Rosenblatt, "She's more dimensional than just a recording artist. When I signed her, I thought her boundaries were limitless. She could become like a Barbara Streisand for this generation. She'll be around a long, long time."

SOURCES:

PERIODICALS

Detroit Free Press, May 19, 1985, May 24, 1985.
Mademoiselle, December, 1983.
Newsweek, March 4, 1985.
New York Times, April 14, 1985.
Playboy, September, 1985.
People, March 11, 1985.
Penthouse, September, 1985.
Record, March, 1985.
Rolling Stone, November 22, 1984, May 9, 1985, May 23, 1985.
Spin, May, 1985.
Time, March 4, 1985, May 27, 1985.
Washington Post, November 25, 1985.

—Sidelights by Gary Graff

William McGowan

1927-

PERSONAL: Full name, William George McGowan; born December 10, 1927, in Ashley, Pa.; son of a railroad union organizer. *Education:* King's College, Wilkes-Barre, Pa., B.S., 1952; Harvard University, M.B.A., 1954.

ADDRESSES: Office—MCI Communications Corp., 1133 19th St. N.W., Washington, D.C. 20036.

OCCUPATION: Entrepreneur; communications company executive.

CAREER: Worked in film business in Hollywood, Calif., helping produce movies for Michael Todd and George Skouras; inventor of several electronic devices and founder of a number of electronics and computer firms in the 1960s; MCI Communications Corp., Washington, D.C., chairman and chief executive officer, 1968—. Director of N-Triple-C, Inc.

SIDELIGHTS: William McGowan doesn't seem to mind that people thought he was a little crazy for wanting to challenge American Telephone & Telegraph's comfortable monopoly of the country's telephone system. The costly years of litigation seem to McGowan a small price to pay for the prize of breaking up the AT&T monolithic hold on the telephone marketplace and nourishing a fledgling phone company to a full-grown aggressor in long-distance service. And the fun is just beginning, McGowan says. He has launched an electronic mail service, and is moving into new areas such as cellular mobile phones and the international phone business—all after leaving the business world for an early retirement at the age of 39. "I went all the way around the world in one direction," he told a *Newsweek* reporter, "and then went all the way around again in the other. Then I decided that I preferred the working world."

Born in Ashley, Pennsylvania, in 1927, McGowan grew up in the coal country of eastern Pennsylvania, the son of a railroad union organizer. Working his way through college, he won a scholarship to Harvard Business School, where he gleaned the business knowledge that was to become invaluable to him years later as an entrepreneur. The glamour of Hollywood captured his interest, and he went to work for movie moguls Michael Todd and George Skouras, helping to produce films that included "Oklahoma." But he abandoned the glitter of Hollywood lights for business of a new kind: working with dollars and figures as a management consultant and venture capitalist. He even turned inventor and learned to transform adversity into advantage—a practice that was to serve him well in his battle against AT&T.

One of McGowan's early inventions was an ultrasonic beeping device that he was convinced would be of great benefit to the U.S. Navy. The beeping, he believed, would serve to repel sharks from pilots downed at sea. However,

the device did not work quite as he planned. Instead of fending off the sharks brought in for the demonstration to Navy brass, the beeping prompted the predators to tear the device apart. Undaunted, McGowan wondered whether the Navy would be interested in a shark aphrodisiac.

McGowan launched several firms in electronics and computers, and, retiring a rich man at thirty-nine, took a trip around the world. The trip didn't cure his restlessness for new venture capital opportunities, and he returned to the business environment to scout them out. That was how he happened on a small Illinois-based company that was struggling to enter the communications business. It was building a single microwave radio link between St. Louis and Chicago to carry long-distance telephone calls. Nearly bankrupt, Microwave Communications of America had what McGowan thought were invaluable assets: a method of transmitting calls cheaper by using microwave transmission instead of copper cables, and a chance to challenge AT&T by offering discount long-distance service to corporate customers. "Challenging the monopoly had one irresistible element," McGowan told *Time*. "It had never been done before."

Because he was not an expert on the telephone industry, what others called an impossible task did not deter McGowan. It was simply a matter of logic, he said. "We looked over the papers in the Federal Communications Commission library, and we couldn't find anything that said AT&T had the rights to a monopoly in telephone service," he recalled to *Time.*

For $50,000, McGowan bought half of the fledgling company and has seen the worth of his shares balloon to around $50 million. The company was reincorporated as MCI Communications Corp. After raising $107 million from private investors whom McGowan was able to sell on his revolutionary idea, construction on microwave transmission towers began, paving the way for what McGowan saw as the future highways of long-distance phone service. Anticipating possible regulatory roadblocks, he moved the company headquarters to Washington, where lobbying efforts could be more effectively carried out and the company would be under the watchful eyes of the federal agencies whose approval was essential to give life to MCI. "I didn't concern myself with the technology, just the regulation of the industry," McGowan said in *Time.*

The technology, however, was no insignificant matter. It was the element that sent many long-distance carriers rushing into the market to achieve cost or quality advantages over AT&T. Analysts predict that as the shakeout in the burgeoning long-distance market occurs over the next few years, the key to survival will be owning, rather than leasing, a communications network. McGowan was quick to see the cost and efficiency advantages of microwave radio transmission over copper cable and built a cross-country network of—at last count—more than 14,500 circuit miles, second in size only to AT&T's network. By sending most calls over its own network rather than buying or leasing transmission facilities from AT&T, MCI has kept overhead low and has been able to offer 30 percent to 50 percent reductions in the cost of long-distance service.

Concentrating on the business client, McGowan's first move with his new company was into the high-density, inner-city market. In 1972, MCI rolled out its telephone service to businesses in a few selected high-traffic cities including New York, St. Louis, and Chicago. Expanding its service around the country, MCI beams calls by microwave to about 80 percent of the nation's telephones; to reach their final destination, calls are transferred to local Bell System lines and carried to customers. Remote areas not serviced by the microwave network can be linked up by leased local lines, a practice that has not received the blessing of Bell System officials who have fought the industry upstart.

During the trial for an antitrust suit brought against AT&T by MCI, George Saunders, a senior attorney for Bell, said in the *New York Times* that MCI's business strategy was to " 'skim the cream' off the most profitable long-distance markets while avoiding obligations to serve lesser, out-of-the-way markets," a practice that he said could eventually "lead to price increases for the public."

Before MCI's service could be established, the company filed lengthy pleas with the Federal Communications Commission and entered into court battles with AT&T that became milestones for the growing industry and opened the door for

competition in the long-distance market. In landmark decisions in 1969 and 1971, the FCC broke the Bell System's fifty-year monopoly on the long-distance market by authorizing McGowan's MCI to build facilities that enabled the company to offer long-distance private-line links between St. Louis and Chicago. In 1971, that decision was expanded to allow other competition to enter the private-line long-distance market and battle AT&T for a share of its 85 million customers. In the 1971 decision, AT&T was ordered by the FCC to provide local facilities for other long-distance companies to use to complete long-distance calls. For McGowan, who compared MCI's challenge to Bell as "a flea crawling up the leg of an elephant" in *Newsweek* magazine, the early FCC victories were just the first shots in an all-out war against AT&T.

Following the FCC's 1971 decisions, MCI began fighting the Bell System for the intracity connections it needed to complete the long-distance calls that moved over the MCI microwave network from city to city. Without the vital connections, MCI could not offer the advantages over AT&T that it had promised. In 1975, AT&T acquiesced to a court order and reluctantly provided the connections—but not before McGowan vowed that his company would be compensated for the lost business in those four years. In a landmark suit that finally sprung open the hinges on AT&T's monopoly and precipitated the breakup of the Bell System, McGowan filed against giant AT&T for $900 million in damages. In 1980, a twelve-member jury in the Chicago Federal District Court found the Bell System guilty of dragging its feet and illegally delaying action on the MCI requests for local connections. The jury awarded MCI $1.8 billion in damages, the largest antitrust judgement in the country's history. McGowan had his day in court and won against a formidable opponent. "Smaller companies that get stepped on by larger companies will come to realize that it is not true that nothing can be done," he told *Newsweek.* "Big companies can no longer beat them by deep-pocketing them." He added in the *New York Times,* "We see in this award the jury saying that they will not allow the largest corporation in the world to use its power to stifle competition."

McGowan found success in the courtroom arena, but he faces some serious challenges ahead in an industry that will test the strength and tenacity of his company. New competition for the consumer's long-distance dollar, in the form of both regional and national long-distance carriers, has crowded the market-place. To keep pace with a quickly-changing industry, MCI has increased its spending for new equipment and technology. In 1984, McGowan pumped more than $20 million a week into new equipment to open up new cities, and he plans to keep the company growing by investing $1 billion a year into expansion. Some of the money will be invested in fiber optic cables, which can be laid next to railroad beds and form links across the country that are efficient and are considered to be state-of-the-art. Adding satellite transponders to the network to quickly and clearly beam calls up from one city and down to the next, McGowan hopes to keep the future success of his company firmly entrenched in its own switches, cables, and microwave towers. "If you own your own system you control your future," McGowan said in *Business-Week.*

New areas such as cellular radio, electronic mail, and nationwide paging are also feeling the support of McGowan's dollars as MCI broadens its business strategy in response to heightened long-distance competition. In 1983, McGowan launched MCI Mail, an electronic mail service conveying information between computers and also to customers without computers who can receive the letters on paper. Through an agreement formulated with the Purolater Inc. courier service, printed messages are delivered within four hours of submission. And, as with MCI's long-distance service, the key to marketing the electronic mail was to sell a better product at a lower price than competitors. "We're going to have to explain our system and make sure that people understand that it's something very different from anything else they've ever seen," McGowan said in *Business-Week* when the service debuted. "We're not in the micro-wave business or any other specialization," he said. "We're in the communications business, and the customer doesn't care—nor should he care—how we send his message."

Whether the infusion of capital, moving into new areas such as cellular mobile phones and electronic mail, and fortifying the existing MCI long-distance network will be sufficient to keep the company predicting a bright future may best be seen in the next few years as long-distance companies feed on others or are gobbled up themselves. With the spread of equal access to connecting lines among all carriers, an industry upset has begun, analysts say.

Mary Johnston, analyst with the Yankee Group in Boston, predicts that by the time equal access is complete in late 1986, the number of long-distance carriers will have sharply decreased to no more than six national carriers like MCI and about thirty "niche market carriers" that will provide specific services or serve a defined geographic area. The connection fees of the long-distance calls, called access charges, have been paid by the long-distance carriers to local phone companies. But as all carriers get equal connections and the additional digits of specialized access numbers disappear, costs of long-distance service may rise because MCI and other cut-rate carriers will no longer have the access-charge discount they have enjoyed. Analysts expect AT&T's costs and rates to decrease, while MCI may have to raise prices. In 1987, when both MCI and AT&T pay similar fees to local phone companies, the competitive edge will belong to the lowest-cost carrier. Where this will leave McGowan and MCI, some say, is behind AT&T. But other industry sources believe that MCI's edge of an efficient network and lower labor costs will keep the company in a strong market position and stable financial future.

Siding with the optimistic outlook, McGowan continues to dream up competitive strategies for MCI that he believes will position the company in the forefront of the telecommunications field. MCI, he believes, will not only continue to underprice AT&T, but will steal its customers away as low costs and efficiency flow over the lines of his long-distance network. "What's significant is that we will finally have a level playing field with AT&T," McGowan said in the *New York Times*. "And we'll be able to attract as much business as we can handle." This translates to what the aggressive entrepreneur once told *Time* magazine his company really stood for: "Money coming in."

SOURCES:

PERIODICALS

Business Week, October 10, 1983, November 5, 1984.
Forbes, January 30, 1980.
New York Times, October 8, 1976, July 18, 1979, June 13, 1980, June 15, 1980, June 16, 1980, February 12, 1984.
Newsweek, June 23, 1980, July 25, 1983.
Time, February 23, 1981, January 7, 1985.

—Sidelights by Amy C. Bodwin

Josef Mengele

1911-1979

OBITUARY NOTICE: Born March 16, 1911, in Guenzburg, Bavaria, Germany (now West Germany); drowned after suffering a stroke while swimming, February 7, 1979, in Bertioga, Brazil; buried in Embu, Brazil; remains were disinterred for medical identification, June 6, 1985. Physician. Mengele became interested in Alfred Rosenberg's theories of Aryan racial superiority while a philosophy student in Munich during the 1920s and later, during his medical studies at the University of Frankfurt am Main, began to formulate his own theories about the possibility of breeding humans to produce a race of Aryan giants.

Mengele enlisted in the German Army in 1939 and joined the Waffen-SS as a medical officer. In 1943, Gestapo chief Heinrich Himmler named Mengele chief medical officer at the Auschwitz-Birkenau concentration camp, where Mengele's duties included determining which incoming prisoners would be assigned to work details and which would be sent to death in the gas chambers. Mengele also devised ghastly medical experiments to perform on the camp's inmates, usually without the benefit of anesthetics. These included the sewing together of children to produce artificial Siamese twins, injecting dye into childrens' eyes to change their eye color, and ripping the limbs from living children. Known as the Angel of Death among the camp's inmates, he is estimated to have been responsible for the deaths of 400,000 people between the time of his arrival at Auschwitz in 1943 and his disappearance in December, 1944.

After World War II Mengele became a prime target for Nazi hunters seeking to bring war criminals to justice. But despite being within the grasp of the Allies several times, Mengele reportedly made his way from a British internment hospital to Rome, where he secured false identity documentation, to South America. Over the course of the next forty years Mengele was the subject of an ongoing manhunt. The search ended in 1985 when an Austrian-born couple, Wolfram and Liselotte Bossert, told Brazilian police that they had sheltered Mengele for several years prior to his death during a swimming holiday in 1979. They said that Mengele had used the cover name Wolfgang Gerhard.

Following disinterment of the remains, a team of international medical and document experts examined the body believed to be Mengele's and compared it to Mengele's service medical records. The team's preliminary report stated that the skeleton unearthed in Brazil was "within a reasonable scientific certainty" that of Mengele. The scien-

UPI/Bettmann Newsphotos

tific report was backed by handwriting analysis, dental and radiological findings, and the testimony of members of Mengele's family.

SOURCES:

BOOKS

Encyclopedia of the Third Reich, McGraw, 1976.

PERIODICALS

Chicago Tribune, June 19, 1985, June 22, 1985, June 23, 1985, June 30, 1985.
Detroit Free Press, June 12, 1985.
New York Times, June 7, 1985, June 10, 1985, June 11, 1985, June 19, 1985, June 20, 1985, June 22, 1985, June 23, 1985, June 27, 1985.

Issey Miyake

1939-

PERSONAL: Name originally Kazunaru Miyake; born April 22, 1939, in Hiroshima, Japan. *Education*: Attended Tama Art University, Tokyo, Japan, 1959-63, and La Chambre Syndicale de la Couture Parisienne, Paris, France, 1965.

ADDRESSES: *Office*—3-5-27 Roppongi, Minato-ku, Tokyo, Japan.

OCCUPATION: Fashion designer.

CAREER: Assistant designer for couturiers Guy Laroche, Paris, France, 1966-68, and Hubert de Givenchy, Paris, 1968-69; designer for Geoffrey Beene, New York City, 1969-70; independent designer, 1970—, director of Miyake Design, Issey Miyake & Associates, Miyake On Limits, and Issey Miyake International, all Tokyo, Japan, and Issey Miyake Europe, Paris, and Issey Miyake U.S.A., New York City. Exhibitions of his work have appeared at Seibu Museum of Art, Tokyo, 1977, Musee des Arts Decoratifs, Paris, 1978, Massachusetts Institute of Technology, Cambridge, Mass., 1982, and San Francisco Museum of Modern Art, 1983; permanent collections housed at Metropolitan Museum of Art, New York City, and Victoria and Albert Museum, London, England.

AWARDS, HONORS: Japan Fashion Editors' Club award, 1974; Mainichi Design Prize, 1977; Pratt Institute award for creativity in design, 1979.

WRITINGS: *Issey Miyake: East Meets West*, edited by Kazuko Koide and Ikko Tanaka, [Tokyo], 1978; *Issey Miyake: Bodyworks*, edited by Shozo Tsurumoti, [Tokyo], 1983.

SIDELIGHTS: Issey Miyake's first name means "one life" in Japanese. And, as if influenced by his name, this internationally-renowned innovator in clothing design displays a remarkable zest and originality in his philosophy and his creations.

After studying art for four years in Tokyo, Miyake set out for the fashion capital of the world—Paris. There he trained in the techniques of couture under famous designers Hubert de Givenchy and Guy Laroche, as assistant designer. Miyake confesses that the ideas behind his original work were formed primarily from the dynamic atmosphere in Paris from 1966 to 1969. Politically active university students in Paris were rebelling against established authority, and the music they listened to reflected their attitude of protest against traditional mores. "Every night, parties! I was so influenced by Janis Joplin, Jimi Hendrix", Miyake told Kennedy Fraser of the *New Yorker*.

© 1983 Eiji Miyazawa/Black Star

Miyake went on to complete his apprenticeship in couture under designer Geoffrey Beene in New York City. He was deeply moved by what he terms the "jeans revolution" brought about by American youth of that era. "Every day I was so *excited*," he recalled to Fraser. "I saw then what it could be—modern life."

"I feel very lucky to have lived when the class system began to crumble, when jeans became the garment for all people," Miyake stated in the *Christian Science Monitor*. "I'm not negative about European couture, but I find clothes of that tradition to be a package that people step into. They are fine and beautiful clothes, but they feel stiff and everyone looks the same in them. . . . I want the body of the wearer, her individuality to make the shape of clothes."

In 1970, Miyake went back to Tokyo to go into business for himself. He worked to develop his own style—a style that would represent modern Japan. "I respect European tradition, but the Europeans do it better," Miyake told Jay Cocks of *Time*. So Miyake drew from his own Japanese tradition. He borrowed the quilted cotton cloth, called *sashiko*, from the Japanese fishermen, farmers, and judo experts. Then he changed the fabric to make it wider, softer, and more sensuous. "It was my denim," Miyake told *Time*.

Miyake also modernized the kimono concept, critics have observed. He took single, rectangular spans of cloth (red silk is one outstanding example) and draped them over his models in freeform fashion. Hilary DeVries noted in the *Christian Science Monitor* that Miyake has raised "the 'wrap and tie' style of dressing beyond mere ethnicity to sophisticated international style that allows the wearer great flexibility." In *Newsweek*, Douglas Davis observed that the designer "opens up space—freedom, in effect for the wearer to reform herself or himself."

Miyake's first Paris show was held in 1973, and he has introduced nearly every collection there since then. But, he stated in the *Christian Science Monitor*, "I hope I am the first and last Japanese designer to have to make my reputation in Paris."

The couturier went on to design cotton jumpsuits reminiscent, in Jay Cocks's view, of *origami*, the traditional oriental art of paper folding. Similarly, Miyake made jerseys out of a ceremonial striped cloth the Japanese used to lead horses. And he transformed the *tanzen*, a Japanese housecoat, into a wool coat with a hood, Cocks reported.

Other Miyake collections have featured "play clothes" such as 1977's boxing trunks and one-piece swim suits with the legs cut high on the thigh. Cover-ups for the latter included skirts, capes, and kimonos. During the same season, Miyake's "bat-winged tops, ballooning pants and loose gauzy dresses, sometimes in two layers," were more "manageable" than in previous years, noted Bernadine Morris in the *New York Times*.

In his 1978 showing, Miyake was "concerned with Japan versus New York," creating "an Oriental view of life in New York City," observed Mary Russell in the *New York Times*. The result was a combination of "kabuki panache and Sony-type organization."

In 1979, Miyake broke tradition and presented his fashions in Milan, Italy, rather than in Paris. Morris commented that Miyake "enlivened things with his Parisian-type presentation." Circumstances brought out his on-the-spot innovative talents when seventeen pairs of pants didn't make it for the show. Miyake simply had the tops modeled over tights. As Morris put it, "the miniskirt was reborn."

The 1980 Miyake collection was shown back in Paris, as were the designs of Claude Montana, Jean Claude de Luca, Castelbajac, Thierry Mugler, and others. Morris wrote in the *New York Times* that "Miyake has style and knows how to make clothes. His show was the best of the day." Morris was not impressed by a "rigid breastplate" of Miyake's design. But she noted that the designer "had some good quilted coats, knitted mini dresses and double tunics of cotton that he meant as dresses. His triangular knee coverings over leg warmers were amusing."

Newsweek writer Jill Smolowe called the Japanese designs of 1982 "bold, flamboyant, even revolutionary. Some are provocative, like Issey Miyake's wool jersey dresses that seem to peel away from the body as a woman moves." Smolowe described Miyake's Issey Sport (now I.S.) collection as "audacious," with inventive combinations like wool and cotton, and the surprise of "magenta zigzags under black flaps."

Miyake's designs for spring, 1984, were called his best up until that time. Featured were "unusual textiles," which included "whisker linen," "cotton embossed by plucking thread," "six-layered woven cotton," and "Japanese paper [raincoat] coated with panlownia oil," reported Hilary DeVries in the *Christian Science Monitor*.

Miyake is regarded as leading the new wave of Japanese designers known as "the Tokyo group." Other members of this coterie include Yohji Yamamoto and Rei Kawakubo, both of design house Comme des Garcons (French for "Like the Boys"). Jenifer Fornaris, who manages a boutique in Rome, told *Newsweek* that this group's "ability, creativity and originality is staggering." Jay Cocks further observed in *Time* that the Japanese designers' clothes "are easy to wear, eccentric only at their most extreme and flattering because they seem to relax around the wearer, not enveloping, containing or constraining the body, but rather exalting its freedom."

Because of the contributions this group has made to the clothing design industry, "Made in Japan" labels on apparel now represent quality rather than mass-production, as they once did, points out Jill Smolowe in *Newsweek*. "Japanese garments have developed a reputation for excellence, from the originality of their fabrics to the durability of their stitchery."

Issey Miyake International is flourishing under the following three labels: Issey Miyake, I.S., and Plantation. The company's gross of $60 million in sales in 1983 represented a 20 percent increase over 1982. In the United States, Miyake's cotton shirts begin at about $50.00. The price tag on a jacket or coat reads around $800.00 (prices quoted in 1983).

Miyake is democratic when it comes to selecting models for his new designs. "I like very much to use real people to show my clothes," Miyake confided to Kennedy Fraser of the *New Yorker*. He often draws from his wide, diverse circle of friends and associates. Whether friends or professional models appear in his shows, Miyake's presentations are "considered unequaled in their theatricality," writes Hilary DeVries in the *Christian Science Monitor*.

The designer himself, however, is a remarkably untheatrical man, thriving in a generally flamboyant milieu. DeVries observed that, dressed in subdued versions of his designs, Miyake "is charming and delightfully unaffected." He has, she said, a "winning personality."

Miyake observed that his idealogy and drive for success developed from the fact that he was born in Hiroshima in the 1930's. "Japan is a very conformist society," he explained in the *Christian Science Monitor*. Miyake and his peers grew up in the "postwar chaos when American and European cultural influences were very great. It hurt me so much not to be proud to be Japanese." It was during this period that Miyake felt compelled to contribute something to the international arena in a way unique and from Japan. "Had I been born 10 or 15 years later, I would not have had as many challenges, but undoubtedly my work would be different," said Miyake.

Designing clothes appears to be not only an expression of idealogy for Miyake, but also of art. He's gifted with an "unparalleled feeling for texture, mass, and volume," noted DeVries in the *Christian Science Monitor*. Critics have likened him to a sculptor, and Miyake himself has said that designing for him is much like "molding clay."

Miyake told Kennedy Fraser of the *New Yorker* that he's "very much influenced by Rauschenberg and Christo as artists—how they think excites me," he said. Commenting about art and the body, Miyake stated: "For me, the body is the most important part of fashion. What I learned in Paris is how the body is beautiful. In Japanese culture, the kimono conceals, transforms the body in a spiritual and philosophical way, makes a package."

But Miyake does not stop with art and philosophy and haute couture. He believes in reaching as many people as he can with his ideas. Miyake innovates for the ready-to-wear market as a way of expressing his democratic views. In addition, he provides new styles of company uniforms and ballet costumes, and he's come out with a line of bed linens.

SOURCES:

PERIODICALS

American Craft, October-November 1983.
Christian Science Monitor, December 15, 1983.
Harper's Bazaar, March 1983.
House and Garden, June 1983.
Metropolitan Home, March 1984.
Newsweek, November 8, 1982, October 17, 1983, April 9, 1984.
New York, March 22, 1982.
New Yorker, December 19, 1983.
New York Times, April 4, 1976, April 6, 1976, October 26, 1976, March 28, 1977, April 10, 1977, October 24, 1977, November 11, 1977, November 27, 1977, April 2, 1978, March 29, 1979, March 31, 1980.
New York Times Magazine, January 30, 1983.
Time, August 1, 1983.
Vogue, May 1984.

—*Sidelights by Victoria France Charabati*

Eugene Ormandy

1899-1985

OBITUARY NOTICE: Real name, Jeno Blau; born November 18, 1899, in Budapest, Hungary; died of pneumonia following a long illness, March 12, 1985, in Philadelphia, Pa. Conductor and music director. Considered one of the world's greatest conductors, Eugene Ormandy led the Philadelphia Orchestra for forty-four years, the longest tenure of any conductor in American history. Gifted with perfect pitch, Ormandy displayed his musical talent at a very early age. A violin prodigy at three, he entered the Budapest Royal Academy when he was five, the youngest student admitted. He received his B.A. at the age of fourteen and soon began performing in concerts across Europe. Ormandy came to the United States in 1921, having been promised a $30,000 concert tour. The tour never materialized; Ormandy, penniless and desperate, took a job as second violinist with the house orchestra at New York's Capitol Movie Theater. He was soon promoted to concertmaster and, in 1924, to conductor. This position led to several free-lance engagements, which prompted Ormandy to resign from the theater orchestra and hire an agent. He conducted for various radio programs and traveled the summer outdoor concert circuit until 1931, when he substituted for guest conductor Arturo Toscanini at the Philadelphia Orchestra. Ormandy's performance led to a five-year contract with the Minneapolis Symphony as conductor and music director.

Ormandy formally joined the Philadelphia Orchestra in 1936, serving as associate conductor with Leopold Stokowski. He was named music director two years later and became the symphony's sole conductor upon Stokowski's departure in 1941. Stokowski left behind a highly disciplined ensemble, noted for its sonorous, electric style. Ormandy not only preserved his predecessor's legacy, he refined and intensified it, creating the widely celebrated "Philadelphia sound." Under Ormandy's direction the orchestra became internationally famous for its virtuosity and tonal richness. He was regarded as a demanding conductor, able to perceive the slightest error. The *London Times* described him as "a ferocious but good humoured slave-driver whose perfection demanded as much from him as from the players he controlled." Ormandy led the symphony on extensive concert tours, performing throughout the United States, Latin America, Europe, Japan, and the People's Republic of China. He retired in 1980 and was made the Philadelphia Orchestra's conductor laureate. Ormandy became a U.S. citizen in 1927. He received numerous awards and honors throughout his career, including the Presidential Medal of

AP/Wide World Photos

Freedom, the Order of the British Empire, and the French Legion of Honor.

SOURCES:

BOOKS

Current Biography, Wilson, 1941.

PERIODICALS

London Times, March 13, 1985.
Newsweek, March 25, 1985.
New York Times, March 13, 1985.
Time, March 25, 1985.
Washington Post, March 13, 1985.

Peter H. Pocklington

1941-

PERSONAL: Born November 18, 1941, in Regina, Saskatchewan, Canada; son of Basil B. (an insurance salesman) and Eileen (Dempsey) Pocklington; married Eva McAvoy, June 2, 1974; children: two sons, two daughters. *Education:* Attended schools in London, Ontario.

ADDRESSES: Office—2500 Sun Life Place, 10123 99 St., Edmonton, Alberta, Canada T5J 3H1.

OCCUPATION: Business executive.

CAREER: Management trainee, Robert Simpson Co. (department store), Toronto, Ontario; salesman and president of car dealerships in Tilbury, Ontario, 1967-69, Chatham, Ontario, 1969-71, and Edmonton, Alberta, 1971-82; chairman of Pocklington Financial Corp. Ltd. Acquired Edmonton Oilers hockey team, 1976, Gainers Ltd. meat packing, 1977, Fidelity Trust, 1979, Swift Canada, 1980, Capri Drilling, 1981, Edmonton Trappers Triple-A baseball team, 1981, and Oakland Stompers professional soccer team.

MEMBER: London (Ontario) Hunt and Country Club, Primrose Club (Toronto), Mayfair Golf and Country Club (Edmonton).

SIDELIGHTS: Tycoon Peter Pocklington has puzzled Canada's normally conservative business community for years. During the 1970s, he cut a high-rolling swath through the pin-striped financial world, quickly expanding a modest used car dealership into a business empire worth more than $1.4 billion. Then, just as quickly, his empire collapsed and he had to sell off many of his holdings. But no one is counting Peter Pocklington out. He is currently retrenching and claimed in a recent interview to still have a personal fortune of between $60 and $100 million.

At the height of his success, Pocklington was one of the richest men in Canada. Former U.S. president Gerald Ford sat on the board of one of his companies. He had a jet-setter's lifestyle and movie stars as friends. But Pocklington wasn't satisfied with his fortune in real estate, investments, meat-packing, and oil. Instead, living out the fantasies of a self-made man, he began turning his attention to the higher profile pursuits of sports and politics. In the process, he blew more than $1 million of his own money in a run for the leadership of the federal Progressive Conservative party and much more than that in questionable business decisions.

Ironically, his sports interests have served him well. He admits he bought the National Hockey League's Edmonton Oilers for an "ego trip" and not a financial investment. But the Oilers' high-flying on-ice performance has turned the franchise into a hot property. Led by superstar Wayne Gretzky, the Oilers have earned Pocklington two successive Stanley Cup victories.

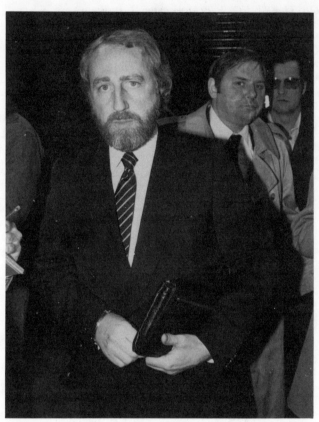

UPI/Bettmann Newsphotos

Pocklington, or Peter Puck as he is commonly known, is hardly a typical entrepreneur. Canadian author and broadcaster Peter Gzowski described him as the "man who would be king." In an infamous 1983 lawsuit, a clairvoyant he hired described him as "power-mad." But no matter what troubles have befallen him on his roller-coaster ride to success, Pocklington has remained completely confident. That is the hallmark of his career. As Gzowski wrote in *Saturday Night,* "Whatever he does, he does with gusto, chortling with pleasure, exclaiming on the excellence of the wine or his good fortune, and punctuating his conversation with cries of self-congratulation."

The son of a London, Ontario insurance salesman, Pocklington showed early signs of the *chutzpah* that was to mark his later business career. When he was a preschooler, he collected chestnuts from a neighbor's lawn and then tried to sell the nuts back to the owner. In his search for riches, he even sold his Christmas presents. And he convinced a group of friends to help him tear down a family barn and sell the wood for cash. The purchase and sale of cars would later become Pocklington's springboard to the business world. And, typically, he had an early education. One weekend while his parents were away, the young Pocklington unloaded the family car for $2,800 and a 1956 Plymouth. Although his parents were at first annoyed with the unauthorized trade, the subsequent sale of the Plymouth earned them an unexpected $800.

After quitting school at age 17, he tried a short stint as a management trainee with the Robert Simpson Co. department store in Toronto. He left the job with the characteristic declaration that he was worth ten times what Simpson would pay. After an early success with a couple of Eastern car dealerships, he pulled up stakes and moved to Alberta just as the oil boom was beginning. Pocklington would later say the lessons he had learned in the car business applied to every other enterprise. "It's all just selling cars, only with more zeroes," Pocklington told one interviewer.

By 1972, Pocklington began toying with real estate, making quick resales in both the American and Canadian markets. He continued to dabble until he crossed paths with one of Canada's fastest and slickest dealers—Nelson Skalbania. One realtor told *Alberta Report* magazine: "What Skalbania did was take a guy who was kind of ambitious, and that was Pocklington, and introduce him to the big game, rolling over this and rolling over that." And roll over he did. He purchased a jet boat company, a ski resort, a large Ford dealership in Toronto, and interests in Pop Shoppe International Ltd. In the fall of 1976, Pocklington purchased the Oilers from Skalbania, even though he had only seen one professional hockey game in his life. He got lost on his first trip to the Northlands Coliseum as owner of the team. In addition, he acquired a Triple-A baseball team, the Edmonton Trappers, and a professional soccer team, the Oakland Stompers.

Pocklington began to expand and diversify his portfolio with the purchase of the Edmonton-based meat packer Gainers Ltd. He confessed at the time that all he knew about food processing was "that cows went in one end and steaks came out the other." By October, 1980, he had acquired the Canadian holdings of Chicago-based Swift and Co. With the merger of Swift and Gainers, Pocklington formed Canada's third-largest packing business. In the fall of 1979, he purchased what would become the centerpiece of his financial empire—Fidelity Trust, an investment firm founded in 1909. He then formed Patrician Land Corp. as a subsidiary of Fidelity. Although he was expanding in various directions, all of his holdings had one common denominator—they had title to valuable real estate.

With his financial success came celebrity. He counted film stars like Paul Newman among his friends. He, his wife Eva, and their son lived in a Tudor-style mansion, complete with seven bathrooms and a collection of Renoir prints. He drove a vintage Rolls Royce convertible to work every morning. "He works harder at having fun than most men do at their jobs," Gzowski noted in *Saturday Night*. But with celebrity came notoriety. In the spring of 1981, Pocklington was wounded in a shoot-out between police and a man who had attempted to kidnap him and his wife. He recovered fully and, indeed, allowed television reporters to interview him from his hospital bed. And in 1983, a clairvoyant named Rita Burns sued Pocklington for $7 million, claiming he had promised her ten percent of the money he invested on her advice. She told a breathless public that he had taken LSD

and that he stood before a mirror every morning and told himself, "I am a god." A jury later dismissed her suit.

But even notoriety had its good points, according to this disciple of positive thinking. "We all have a few skeletons in the closet," the *Globe and Mail* quoted Pocklington as saying after his lawsuit victory. "If we got them all out we'd have quite a party." Pocklington is the embodiment of positive thinking. During his first year as owner of the Oilers, he insisted that all team members attend self-development seminars operated by a California institute. He often told friends and workers that they could do anything if they put their minds to it. But for Pocklington—the self-made man—positive thinking finally became wishful thinking when he decided to become Prime Minister of Canada.

Like many businessmen, he was convinced his skills could apply just as well to government as to the marketplace. Although he had earlier supported Prime Minister Pierre Trudeau, he believed the Liberal policies that had resulted in a high federal deficit and massive unemployment were inexcusable. He wanted to replace "the amateurs running the business of the country." So he submitted his name as a candidate in the June, 1983, leadership contest for the Progressive Conservative party.

For Pocklington, the political world was a simple place. The solutions to complex policy problems were made easy when business principles were applied. A good prime minister, he believed, would sell off Canada's crown corporations. He also proposed a flat twenty percent tax for all taxpayers earning more than $12,000. Many observers, however, found it difficult to take Pocklington's musings seriously. He had no background in public service. And he wasn't proposing a conventional route to political office; rather he aimed to take a direct stab at the top. Liberal senator and power broker Keith Davey said the world of politics was too sophisticated to offer itself up to Pocklington's ambitions. And Peter Lougheed, Alberta's Conservative premier and acquaintance of Pocklington, publicly dismissed him as a viable political alternative. The simple world of politics, however, was about to become complicated for Peter Pocklington. He launched his campaign by stating he would divorce himself from all business interests except his sports franchises. Yet financial troubles struck at precisely the same moment.

Public records showed that Pocklington's companies borrowed heavily during 1982 and early 1983 at high interest rates. A telling blow was struck when Fidelity Trust faltered. In early 1983, during the leadership campaign, it was revealed that Fidelity had exceeded a federally set 20-to-1 borrowing guideline because its asset base, largely real estate, had withered. A federal agency placed the company on a one-week operating license rather than the normal one-year permit. Pocklington had to inject $20.6 million of new capital into the company or find a new owner. When he couldn't come up with the money or a buyer, the government asked for management proposals from several companies to safeguard Fidelity's $840 million in public deposits. In late June, federal regulators appointed Vancouver-based First Trust as new manager of the trust company.

The man who would be prime minister suffered further embarrassment when his major car dealership was placed in receivership and his meat-packing company was reduced in size. It was clearly becoming difficult for Pocklington to base his leadership campaign on the strength of his business acumen. In addition, fellow right-wing Conservatives had trouble with many of his political ideas and dubbed his flat-tax proposal "a political nightmare." Pocklington was defeated on the first ballot of the leadership vote but showed some political savvy by crossing the floor to support the eventual winner and new prime minister, Brian Mulroney.

Observors began to write Pocklington off. He had, after all, seen $75 million of his own personal fortune slip through his fingers. But Pocklington continued to surprise the business community. Armed with his own sense of confidence, he began to rebuild. The road back wasn't easy. He had to give up the private Lear jet and the personal office chef. The Rolls Royce was traded in for a more modest Mercedes Benz. And he had to use his beloved Oilers as collateral for loans with a bank and later with the Alberta government.

In 1981 his companies had assets of $1.4 billion and sales of $900 million. In 1985 he reduced his portfolio to five companies with assets of $150 million and projected sales of $475 million. Pocklington has nevertheless maintained his old enthusiasm. In an interview with Robert Sheppard of the Toronto *Globe and Mail,* he said rumors of his demise were greatly exaggerated. "When you are worth between $60 and $100 million, you are not dead yet." He referred to his political debacle as "a great learning process. Truly, one of the highlights of my life." Pocklington still hopes Prime Minister Mulroney will recognize his talents and appoint him to head a royal commission to study tax laws. And he has steadfastly refused to part with the Oilers, despite several offers.

Pocklington once told *Maclean's* magazine: "This world seems to judge people on 'God, if you take a gamble and you lose, Holy Lord, you're a crook,' rather than 'Thank God, people take gambles and occasionally win and occasionally lose.' " Peter Pocklington clearly is a man who has lived by his philosophy.

AVOCATIONAL INTERESTS: Boat racing, skiing.

SOURCES:

BOOKS

Newman, Peter C., *The Acquisitors,* McClelland & Stewart, 1981.

PERIODICALS

Alberta Report, July 19, 1982, August 8, 1983, October 17, 1983, April 9, 1984.
Financial Post, April 2, 1983.
Maclean's, April 18, 1983.
Saturday Night, April, 1982.
Toronto Globe and Mail, May 16, 1983, September 29, 1983, October 19, 1983, January 28, 1985.
Toronto Life, January, 1984.
Winnipeg Free Press, October 6, 1982, October 20, 1982, October 22, 1982.
Winnipeg Sun, April 5, 1983.

—Sidelights by Ingeborg Boyens

Anna Maximilian Potok

1907-

BRIEF ENTRY: Full name, Anna Maximilian Apfelbaum Potok; born June 4, 1907, in Warsaw, Poland. Polish-American fur designer. The president of Maximilian Furs, Inc. since 1953, Anna Maximilian Potok is considered the doyenne of international furriers. Over the years she has designed furs for numerous wealthy and prominent women from around the world, including Queen Elizabeth, the Duchess of Windsor, Nancy Reagan, Jacqueline Kennedy Onassis, Diana Ross, and Marilyn Monroe.

Potok's career began in Warsaw in 1922 when she joined her brother's thriving fur salon. Potok and her brother, Maximilian Apfelbaum, along with her husband and son, fled Poland in 1939, shortly before the Nazi invasion. The family settled in New York, where Potok and Apfelbaum opened a small shop on Fifth Avenue. In 1940 they moved their business to its present location on West 57th Street. Fashion mavens Diana Vreeland and Helena Rubinstein were early, enthusiastic customers; with their support, Maximilian Furs quickly became the preferred furrier among royalty, heads of state, and celebrities.

Jack Manning/NYT Pictures

Potok assumed full control of the family operation upon her brother's death in 1961. Although she is nearing eighty, Potok has no plans to retire. "To the last minute of my life, I'll be in business," she told Harriet Shapiro of *People*. The *New York Times*'s Enid Nemy reports that age is of little consequence to the designer. "I think every day that today was good but tomorrow must be better, not only in business but for myself," Potok explains. "Every day has been a challenge from childhood on." *Address:* Maximilian Furs, Inc., 20 West 57th St., New York, N.Y. 10019.

SOURCES:

PERIODICALS

New York Times, April 5, 1982.
People, February 1, 1982.

Karen Ann Quinlan

1954-1985

OBITUARY NOTICE: Born March 29, 1954; died of respiratory failure due to acute pneumonia, June 11, 1985, in Morris Plains, N.J. Quinlan, who had been severely comatose since 1975, made legal and medical history in 1976 when a unanimous decision by the New Jersey Supreme Court allowed the removal of her life-support systems. The landmark "right-to-die" ruling made Quinlan "a symbol of the right of the terminally ill to decide their fates with their families," according to a *Chicago Tribune* report.

A former athlete and lifeguard who also liked to write poetry and play the piano, Quinlan lapsed into a coma on April 14, 1975, following a birthday celebration for her boyfriend. Doctors believe that her breathing was impaired by a combination of three alcoholic drinks, aspirin, and a "therapeutic" dose of the mild prescription tranquilizer Valium, plus a stringent diet, which consequently deprived her brain of oxygen. The exact cause of the coma, however, has not been conclusively determined. Several other factors may have contributed, Quinlan's adoptive parents said, including her low-blood-sugar condition, a fall on concrete two weeks prior to the birthday party, and possible lead poisoning from a factory job she had held.

Doctors determined after several months that Karen Ann would never return to a "cognitive state." Her parents were distressed, said a *Detroit Free Press* report, because she "was fighting the machine and it caused a great deal of discomfort." In addition, they stated, several years prior to becoming comatose, Karen Ann had expressed a wish never to be kept alive by elaborate life-sustaining means. The Quinlans, who had long given up hope that their daughter would recover, felt that she was suffering needlessly and decided to petition a New Jersey Superior Court judge to allow them to remove the respirator. The petition was denied, but the decision was reversed when the Quinlans appealed it to the New Jersey Supreme Court on March 31, 1976. The Supreme Court ruled that a person's right to privacy allowed the removal of life-supporting equipment and named Mr. Quinlan guardian, responsible for deciding Karen's fate. Death "would not be homicide, but rather expiration from natural causes," the judgment said, and therefore no one could be held criminally liable for disconnecting the respirator.

Unexpectedly, Karen Ann began breathing on her own after the respirator was removed. For ten years she remained

AP/Wide World Photos

alive, but in what was called a permanent vegetative state, never regaining consciousness. Her family continued their devotion to Karen Ann until her death at age thirty-one, and her father drove forty miles daily to visit her in a nursing home. Karen Ann's physical condition deteriorated sharply for several months prior to her death, and she suffered from severe lung infections. In her memory, the Quinlans founded the Karen Ann Quinlan Center for Hope, a hospice for terminally ill patients and their families.

SOURCES:

PERIODICALS

Chicago Tribune, June 13, 1985.
Detroit Free Press, June 12, 1985, June 13, 1985.

Mary Lou Retton

1968-

PERSONAL: Born January 24, 1968, in Fairmont, W.Va.; daughter of Ronnie (owner of a coal transportation business) and Lois Retton. *Education:* Attended high school in Fairmont, W.Va. and took correspondence courses; studied gymnastics with Bela Karolyi in Houston, Tex.

ADDRESSES: Agent—John S. Traetta, National Media Group/High Bar Productions, Ltd., 250 West 57th St., New York, N.Y. 10107.

OCCUPATION: Gymnast.

CAREER: Gymnast since 1975, competing numerous national and international events, including the 1984 Summer Olympics in Los Angeles, Calif. Spokesperson for and endorser of a variety of commercial products and enterprises.

AWARDS, HONORS: Winner of one gold, two silver, and two bronze medals in gymnastics in 1984 Summer Olympics; named Sportswoman of the year by *Sports Illustrated*, 1984.

SIDELIGHTS: On August 3, 1984, gymnast Mary Lou Retton did far more than just win an Olympic gold medal. True, the flawless performance of the four-foot, nine-inch, sixteen-year-old won her a perfect 10 score in the all-around gymnastic category, but at the same time, the perpetual smile and enthusiasm displayed by the girl won her the hearts of all who watched.

AP/Wide World Photos

Her victory was a many-faceted wonder. Mary Lou Retton's performance proved to the world that the United States was a gymnastic force to be reckoned with. She also proved to the gymnastic world that a gymnast need not be needle thin and wisp light. Many observers have been inclined to liken Retton's muscular, solid body more to that of a linebacker than the lithe creatures usually seen passing between the balance beam and uneven bars. Yet her delivery, while decisive, powerful, and daring is no less graceful than any the world has ever seen.

"I vault my best under pressure," she told the *New York Times* after her Olympic victory at UCLA's Pauley Pavilion before a crowd of 9,023. "It makes me fight harder. I knew if I stuck that vault I'd win it. I kept thinking 'stick, stick, stick,' I knew I had to get a 10." To "stick" in gymnastics means to descend from all the midair twisting and turning in perfect form and rock steady. And she did. "I can't describe how I felt," said the 92-pound Retton. "I had goosebumps going up and down me. I knew from the takeoff. I knew from the run—I just knew it."

Retton was born January 24, 1968, in Fairmont, West Virginia, a coal-mining town. She is the youngest of five

children. Her father, Ronnie, owns a coal transportation equipment business and at one time was a New York Yankees farm-team shortstop. Her mother, Lois, started Mary Lou in acrobatic and ballet classes by the time she was four because, as the gymnast told the *New York Times,* "I was very hyper." She started serious gymnastic training when she was seven. At eight, she recalls watching the tiny Nadia Comaneci win three gold medals and countless hearts in the 1976 Olympics, just as thousands of aspiring young gymnasts must now remember watching her.

But perhaps the first tiny gymnast to have the world on a string was Olga Korbut who, at seventeen, reigned over the gymnastic events of the 1972 Munich Olympics. That year there were approximately 15,000 gymnasts practicing in private clubs in the United States, said *Harper's.* In 1982 there were 150,000, many inspired by Korbut. Today, there are over 500 private clubs in this country, and annual fees for gymnasts intent on Olympic competition can run more than $12,000 for tuition, room, gear and travel expenses.

Many of the most serious students leave home at tender, teen ages and move to the homes of teachers in the finer schools. That is what Retton did in early 1983. With her parents' permission she gave up regular high school classes (where she earned straight A's) for correspondence courses, and she left West Virginia to move in with a family who had another gymnast in the same school as the one Retton chose to attend—Karolyi's World Gymnastics. The Houston school is run by Bela Karolyi, the Romanian coach who, with his wife, Marta, instructed Comaneci on her road to fame before the couple defected to the United States in 1981.

Of her decision to leave home Retton told *Time:* "I knew that if I wanted to have a chance at a medal in the Olympics, I was not going to do it if I stayed home. And I had worked all of those long, hard years."

At the school she works out twice daily, except on her off-day, Monday, when the workout takes place only once. She and Karolyi met at a tournament in Reno in 1982. "I immediately recognized the tremendous physical potential of this little kid," Karolyi told *The New York Times.* In comparing his two star pupils, Karolyi told *Newsweek:* "Nadia was a great champion, but Mary Lou is bigger. She's got the psychological power to go through the most difficult moments without falling apart." And in the *New York Times* he said: "Nadia never lifted her eyes. Mary Lou communicates with her crowd."

The *New York Times* best describes Retton's personal best as "an affront to gravity called the Retton flip," in which she swings down from the high bar and slams her hips against the low bar, going into a front flip that ends when she lands in a seated position on the high bar.

Public recognition of Retton's talents first came in March, 1982, when she took top honors at the McDonald's American Cup competition. She was substituting, on a single day's notice, for schoolmate Dianne Durham who had been injured. But the road to fame was not clearly and simply Retton's from the start. After watching the February 5, 1983, Caesars Palace Invitational in Las Vegas, James Wolcott reported in *Harper's* that "it was Mary Lou Retton who looked the most aerodynamically self-propelled. No sylph she, Mary Lou has such a boxy, compact body that some coaches feel that she won't grow gracefully in the sport—that whatever pounds she adds in puberty will be maldistributed. For the time being, however, she's hitting everything with smacking emphasis, ending her routines with an exclamation mark. . . . For her exploits, Mary Lou was awarded first prize in the all-around and presented with an armful of flowers and a trophy nearly as tall as herself. . . . She said 'It feels *great*, and this is my first time, you know at beating the top seniors, and it feels absolutely excellent,' adding 'Name recognition is very important in gymnastics, and I hope this boosts my name right up there, somewhere.' "

Six weeks before the Olympics, Retton suffered an injury that a few years earlier might have sidelined her for the

Mary Lou Retton on the balance beam at the 1984 Summer Olympics. UPI/Bettmann Newsphotos.

competition and left her with a long, slow recuperation. After injuring her right knee during an exhibition match, the knee started locking on her. Examination showed that a cartilage fragment from her knee had broken off and lodged in the joint. She flew to St. Luke's Hospital in Richmond, Virginia for arthroscopy. She checked out the same day as her surgery and was back at practice in Houston the next day, according to *Time.*

At the Olympics, Retton's chief competitor was Ecaterina Szabo, seventeen, of Romania who was the world champion and pre-Olympic favorite. Szabo won gold medals in the floor exercise, the balance beam, and the vault, and she led her group to the team gymnastics title.

In the course of the competition for the all-around gold, Mary Lou took an early .15 lead, but the lead was erased when Szabo scored a 10 on the balance beam, while Retton's weakness on the uneven bars netted her only a 9.85. Retton was down .05 going into the last round of competition. Szabo had to go first on the uneven bars. "I saw her take a step on her dismount," Retton told *Sports Illustrated,*" and I said to myself, 'You have a chance, Mary Lou.' " Szabo scored a 9.9 on the unevens, and it was time for Retton to take on the vault. If she scored 9.95 she would tie for the gold, but a perfect 10 would net her first place all alone.

That is exactly what Retton did; not just once, but twice. Gymnasts go through each routine twice, and the highest score of the two counts. Although Retton scored a perfect 10 on her first vault, she thrilled the partisan Los Angeles crowd by repeating her routine—and her perfect score—a second time.

"Mary Lou has two great qualities that put her where she is," Don Peters, U.S. women's team coach, told the *New York Times.* "First, physically, she is the most powerful gymnast who ever competed in the sport, and she takes great advantage of that in her tumbling and her vaulting. . . . Second, she's one hell of a competitor. As the pressure gets greater, Mary Lou gets greater."

But, as wonderful as the Olympics may have been, Mary Lou and her family are wise enough to know that the fickle public tends to have a short memory. Retton, with the advice of professionals, is taking on a number of lucrative endorsement contracts. Coordinating the campaign that *People* magazine refers to as the "Rettonization of America" is John Traetta, gymnastics coach for ten years at New York's DeWitt Clinton High School, who met Mary Lou three years ago while he was producing a gymnastics special for Caesars Palace. Traetta, president of National Media/ Highbar Productions, is Retton's agent and has signed her to multi-year contracts with McDonald's, General Mills, Wheaties, and Vidal Sassoon. (She is the first woman, and only the third person, to be declared official spokesperson for the "breakfast of champions," although she owns up to preferring Cap'n Crunch cereal.) She has also agreed to endorse a line of girls' sportswear for the Dobie Originals division of Cluett, Peabody & Company and has signed with Hasbro Bradley to promote physical fitness toys for children.

In the four months immediately after the Olympics, Retton toured twenty-eight cities, appearing in parades, shows, and special events. And she was named Sportswoman of the Year for 1984 by *Sports Illustrated.* She is often escorted to functions by her older brother Ronnie, twenty-three, who shares a two-bedroom Houston condominium with her. She visits her family once each month and drives a red Corvette bearing the vanity license plate "Mary Lou" and the five-interlocked-ring Olympic symbol.

Retton continues to be captivating and remains captivated by her fame. "The people knew me!," she told *Sports Illustrated* "They said things like, 'Mary Lou, you've been in our home. You've been in our living room. We feel like we know you, Mary Lou!'. . . . I still think it's kind of neat, too. I mean, I'd understand people recognizing me if I had purple hair or something, but I'm just a normal teenager. I'm still Mary Lou."

And sometimes that can be a lonely person to be. She admits to having little contact with girls her own age, and while she keeps her eyes open for appealing boys, "I really don't have time," she told the *Chicago Tribune.* "You know, I'm still young, and here all of this stuff is happening to me and I have to take advantage of it. Gosh, this opportunity and period of my life may never come back again. There'll be time for boys and partying later."

Retton and other Olympic athletes with endorsement contracts keep their amateur standing by putting their earnings into a trust fund administered by the United States Gymnastics Federation. The organization pays for her training expenses from the fund, and when Retton is ready to give up her amateur status, a percentage of the trust is kept by the association, with the majority of it going to Retton.

From Christmas until March Retton will again be in serious training at Karolyi's school (where *People* says enrollment doubled after Retton's victory), and she is expected to start competing within a year of her last Olympic finale. She will have to decide for herself how long she wants to maintain the amateur status and rigorous schedule that led to the Olympic gold and fame.

SOURCES:

PERIODICALS

Chicago Tribune, March 10, 1985.
Christian Science Monitor, March 22, 1984, August 6, 1984, August 17, 1984, October 25, 1984, October 31, 1984.
Harper's, July 13, 1983.
Newsweek, July 30, 1984, August 13, 1984.
New York Times, March 4, 1984, May 14, 1984, July 31, 1984, August 1, 1984, August 4, 1984, August 5, 1984, September 24, 1984, April 28, 1985.
People, November 28, 1983, August 6, 1984, December 24, 1984.
Sports Illustrated, December 24, 1984.
Time, July 30, 1984, August 20, 1984.

—Sidelights by Mary Solomon Smyka

Mary Sinclair

1918-

PERSONAL: Born September 23, 1918, in Chisholm, Minn.; daughter of Joseph (manager of a school power plant) and Margaret Palcich; married William Sinclair (an attorney), September, 1945; children: John, Peter, Rosemary, Thomas, Ann. *Education:* College of St. Catherine, St. Paul, Minn., bachelor's degree in English and chemistry, 1940; University of Michigan, master's degree in environmental communications, 1973.

ADDRESSES: Home—5711 Summerset, Midland, Mich. 48640.

OCCUPATION: Social activist.

CAREER: Research librarian for Dow Chemical Co., Midland Mich., after graduation from college; associate editor of *Chemical Industries* magazine, New York, N.Y., during World War II; technical writer for Dow Chemical Co.; abstract writer, Library of Congress, Washington, D.C., during the 1950s; freelance writer in Midland; currently social activist, specializing in nuclear power and environmental issues. Lecturer.

SIDELIGHTS: When Mary Sinclair was working for the Library of Congress in Washington, D.C., in the 1950s, she never guessed that some of the documents she was reading on nuclear technology would lead her into battle with a powerful utility company. And she never anticipated the personal price she would pay for a victory.

Born in Chisholm, Minnesota, in 1918, Sinclair now lives in Midland, Michigan, where she and her husband raised five children in the shadow of a nuclear power plant that the local utility, Consumers Power Company, built just a few miles from her home. During her days at the Library of Congress, Sinclair had watched and learned about the emerging technology of nuclear power. And for many years, she supported nuclear power, even though she saw serious problems with the technology that was being promoted by the Atomic Energy Commission as safe, clean, and economical. Sinclair was confident that problems such as waste disposal and radiation leaks would be addressed and a solution would be found. But in 1967, when Consumers Power proposed plans to build a nuclear power plant in Midland, Sinclair realized the problems had not been solved. Her scientific interest in nuclear power quickly turned to personal concern, and in a drive to present facts that she felt were not reaching the public, she turned to activism.

Drawing upon years of science writing and editing, and on her accumulated knowledge of nuclear power, Sinclair began raising issues that she felt the citizens of Midland needed to know. The community's hostile reaction stunned her. Her children received pressure from peers at school, her husband's law practice began losing clients, and she became the

target of harassment, including anonymous phone calls and letters. Her stance against the plant cost her the chance of any employment in Midland, she says. Yet she persisted with her campaign, writing letters to the editor of the Midland *Daily News*, forming the Saginaw Valley Nuclear Study Group, and attempting to persuade government officials and the Michigan Public Service Commission, which regulates utilities in Michigan, that her concerns were valid.

Sinclair fought against (and lost) the construction licensing of the plant, which Consumers Power originally projected to take seven years to complete and cost $350 million. As she lost battles in the courts and in her home town, Sinclair grew more determined to fight the plant. As it was being built, she uncovered evidence of construction problems, safety concerns, and design deficiencies. At the operating licensing hearings for the plant, she presented a list of eighteen reasons why the plant should not be permitted to operate. Her battle slowly gained strength, not only because of increasing concern in surrounding communities, but also because of serious doubts that one of the plant's key supporters was beginning to have. The Dow Chemical Company, which had contracted with Consumers Power to buy power from one of the two nuclear reactor units that were being built, began eyeing construction delays and cost overruns, and reevaluating its contract with Consumers.

Public opinion in Midland slowly began to change, and the *Daily News* praised Sinclair for standing up to ostracism and criticism with courage. The community was beginning to realize that Sinclair's objections might have merit, and she was given credit for prompting public discussion. The Nuclear Regulatory Commission announced it was fining Consumers Power $120,000 for plant construction violations. And when Consumers announced new cost estimates for the plant of more than $4 billion and a completion date in 1985, the utility's biggest customer decided to end its contract. Dow Chemical filed a lawsuit against Consumers to be freed of its contractual liabilities to buy power from the plant, and more than a year later, in July of 1984, Consumers Power abandoned the Midland plant because it was unable to obtain financing. It was scrapped amid intense public criticism, eighty-five percent completed, and at a cost to Consumers Power of $4.9 billion over 13 years.

The plant's towers stand silent over Midland, and Consumers Power is hoping to find a buyer for its costly project. Sinclair says she never expected the plant to be shut down and feels she has scored a victory of sorts over a technology she no longer supports. Her battle at Midland gained her national attention and has placed her on celebrity rolls. She has been interviewed by print media including the *Wall Street Journal, Ms.* magazine, and several Michigan newspapers. Sinclair also was the subject of a segment on the CBS news magazine "60 Minutes." She is modest about her achievements and about being cast into the spotlight; she laughs when asked if she feels like a celebrity. "I guess I'm a celebrity," she told *CN*. "But I don't feel like it."

Continuing to speak out against nuclear power, Sinclair is kept busy with speaking engagements and lectures. She says she would like to sit down some day and write a book but currently does not have the time. She has researched and written letters on alternative energy options but does not plan to abandon her stance on nuclear power and her campaign to change the "old-fashioned thinking" that she says still surrounds nuclear technology. "As long as there's somebody listening, something will happen," Sinclair says.

CN INTERVIEW

CN interviewed Mary Sinclair by telephone at her home in Midland, Mich., in June, 1985.

CN: You worked for the Library of Congress in Washington D. C., in the fifties. Was that when you first started becoming acquainted with atomic energy and with nuclear power plants?

SINCLAIR: I first got some knowledge of the technology, and of course I could tell there were certain problems but nothing too extraordinary. And we were getting reports from other industrial laboratories that had government funding, and university laboratories, and they were discussing problems. So I did learn something about the technology, and I figured they would be *solving* those problems.

CN: So you were supportive of that technology at that time, then?

SINCLAIR: Oh, yes. When I first raised questions, it wasn't with the idea of stopping it, just to make it as safe as possible.

CN: When did your ideas about nuclear technology begin to change?

SINCLAIR: Well, in the mid-sixties, I went back to free-lance writing for the Dow Chemical Company, and I started getting back into studying technical literature—kind of getting caught up. I had always retained a real interest in nuclear power, and at that point I began to read in the technical literature about some of the problems that hadn't been solved. And they were pretty serious. Also, they had identified problems that they certainly didn't know about in the early stages of the development of nuclear power, and there was no answer for those. I thought these were pretty serious issues and that they had better be raised early to make the technology safer.

Among the issues that I was looking at was that the Advisory Committee on Reactor Safeguard, which was the most prestigious group of scientists and engineers in the country that advised the Atomic Energy Commission, were writing to the chairman of the Commission telling him that there was an urgent need for more safety research in the large-sized plants that were then planned for construction—such as the Midland plant—and they spelled out the areas in which more work had to be done. And, furthermore, they were saying in this correspondence, which I had read in the *Congressional Quarterly*, that they had been seeing this for about three years, but nothing came of it. And they were concerned about it. So I thought that certainly if we started some discussion on this in the community it would require our elected representatives to prod the Atomic Energy Commission into *doing* something.

Also, I became aware of the fact that there was serious internal struggle within the Atomic Energy Commission about the adequacy of ratings and standards; and of course there was no solution to the nuclear waste problem. But none of these issues were being presented to the public at all. The promotional literature was saying that nuclear power was safe and economical. On top of that, Dow Chemical was buying the propaganda that the electricity from these plants would be cheaper, and so it was going to hook up the Dow-Midland Division to the nuclear plants. Of course this troubled me a lot, because I could see that the issues that I was looking at—that I thought ought to be handled some way—were coming from very good scientists whom I recognized and respected.

CN: In 1967, when Consumers Power announced the plans for the Midland Plant, what was your initial reaction?

SINCLAIR: I thought that it was a good move. That's before I began to find out the problems. I was quite enthusiastic about it. It was only later that I began to discover what was going on. My initial reaction was very positive.

CN: How was the plant promoted in the community around Midland?

SINCLAIR: They had huge ads in the paper, huge ads on TV, and on the radio; and of course, nationwide, there was a big advertising campaign for the nuclear plants that they were going to build all over the country. They were advertising very heavily throughout that period.

CN: Did you see things in the ads that differed from your knowledge of what would happen with the plants?

SINCLAIR: Well, at first I didn't. I just noticed that the ads were very positive and minimized any problems whatsoever with nuclear plants. There were ads like "Mom's apple pie is radioactive and so is mom. That doesn't make her a dangerous woman." And they were all over, like in the *Reader's Digest* and *Life* magazine. But after I began to learn something about the issues, then I realized how misleading—terribly misleading—the ads were. And yet that was about all the public was hearing in the mass media. The *problems* were only carried in the technical literature that nobody ever sees. So that's why I wanted to raise these issues, and I thought Midland might be the right community in which to raise them, because it is a highly technical community and people would recognize the scientists and the credibility of the sources that were saying these things. I thought that in doing that we could start to correct some of these problems in a pretty orderly way, just by having the community sort of gear into saying they want these problems solved.

CN: Did you anticipate that you would have any trouble convincing the community of the problems or getting the community to work with you?

SINCLAIR: I didn't anticipate—begin to anticipate—the kind of reaction I got. I just wandered into it to tell you the truth. I had no idea that there would be that much hostility or that Midland was so totally a company town. I suppose it isn't too much different from any other company town. Except I never realized just how much that was the mentality here, and I didn't realize just how intense it was. But that's what happened.

And of course after that started I was quite shaken up, but I decided that I knew what I was reading. I had done very difficult technical writing before, and it had always been accepted. And I had worked as an editor on a chemical magazine that was published nationally. By that time I had about ten or twelve years of science writing and editing experience. I knew what I was reading. I knew its significance, and I couldn't back away from it. I also thought my freedom of speech was very important to me, especially on this subject. I intended to discuss issues that could affect my family and my home. These plants were within *one mile* of my husband's office on Main Street and within about two miles of my home. All our lives—and our family's health and well-being—were all tied up right here. So certainly I was going to look into anything I thought could threaten that.

CN: How did you start your campaign or protest against the plants?

SINCLAIR: Well, as I say, the first thing I did was decide to write a letter to the editor of the local newspaper with the ideal that we might be able to get some community discussion going. But the hostile reaction was extraordinary.

I put the letters in the Saginaw/Bay City paper, too, and I had some responses from those places. People said that they were concerned and asked if I would send more information. Some of them sent me a little money—$5 or $10—for the information. As far as Midland was concerned, I tried putting a couple more letters into the paper, and then I also decided to get some more information, thinking, "Maybe there is something I'm missing here."

And it just so happened there was a seminar offered by the State University of New York, outside of Albany on—well, it was on environmental problems, but nuclear pollution was one of the things to be discussed. I think it was one of the earliest environmental seminars. I told my husband, "I've just got to go to that seminar because I'll have a chance to talk to people on the Atomic Energy Commission as well as people from some very good Eastern universities who were on the program. And I'll have a chance to see if there are some facts that I'm missing here." So I went, and I found out I was right. The people from the Atomic Energy Commission said they really didn't know, for example, what the long-term effects would be of low-level radiation that was routinely put into the air and water from the nuclear plants. But they did know that radiation caused cancer, was life-shortening, and, most important of all, caused genetic damage.

The engineers I met there said that they were concerned about what they called "scaling" from very small nuclear power plants—the small nuclear power plants that had been built up to that time—and jumping very quickly to very large-sized plants. What the engineers were saying was that when you scale up quickly like that you can't expect the computer codes designed for the smaller plants to give you accurate information over such a wide span or such an increase in size. You are just not going to get accurate information. I also got some very good papers from that seminar with good bibliographies, so it expanded my base of information, and I felt on very solid ground then for anything I wanted to say. When I got back I decided to start campaigning again, and that's how I got going.

CN: When you said that you had a hostile reaction in the community, what kind of things happened, was it just yourself or was your family affected as well?

SINCLAIR: My children were subjected to peer pressure. Because the other children's parents were upset with what I was saying, my children would be hassled at school. The truth is, I worried a lot about them. They told me later that when they were in high school they had made a pact among themselves not to worry me and tell me what was happening to them, because they knew I was so worried about so many things as it was.

CN: Were you ever able to find any support within the community?

SINCLAIR: Oh, yes. At first I had some people from the surrounding area take an interest. And then, for my first education effort, I sent out about twenty packets of papers I had collected on various issues to about twenty scientists that I knew. In my cover letter I said, "Don't you think you should discuss this now, before the plants are built?" I only got replies from about three of them—two of them were anonymous—and they said, "Well, we know you're right, but we're afraid it might cost us our jobs."

CN: Were you working at the time?

SINCLAIR: I had been free-lance writing for Dow Chemical. After I raised the issue in a very polite way in a letter to the editor I never got another job. It was like I was unemployable. So one of these scientists gave a packet of my information to Dorothy Dow who is the oldest daughter of Herbert Dow, and she came to my door one day and said I had done a good job and that she was very concerned about pollution, too, especially if she was going to be linked with the Midland Division of Dow Chemical, which her father founded. She said that she would pay the copying and mailing costs if I would write a letter to the board of directors and send them the information. She wanted the letter sent to both the board of directors of Dow and the board of directors of Consumers Power Company. I did that, and I got three letters from the board of directors of Dow and nothing at all from Consumers Power.

Since we couldn't get the issues addressed by the board of directors, the only other channel that was left was to enter the licensing hearing and put these questions in a petition. The licensing board is then required to deal with it. I started quite a campaign, and gradually there were citizens—Sierra Club members especially—who took an active interest. We put on a public forum and invited someone from Consumers. They flew in somebody. It was quite well attended. And after that we said that anyone who was interested could join us in what we called the Saginaw Valley Nuclear Safety Group.

CN: You also took your campaign to the Michigan Public Service Commission, the governor, Congressional Representatives.

SINCLAIR: Yes, I kept writing, and they finally told me that they were going to have a hearing and that I would be given fifteen minutes to discuss my views on nuclear power, and they wanted my paper two weeks in advance. At first I said to my husband, "I don't think I'm going to drive ninety miles to Lansing to discuss nuclear power for fifteen minutes. But he just looked at me and said: "You know, if they give you five minutes, go, because that's the process; that's all you've got. And just hope that there is at least one person in that hearing room that is listening and thinks that what you have got to say has some merit." I had never looked at it like that before. I wrote my paper and turned it in, and I found that you can get quite a bit in fifteen minutes if you put your mind to it. So I went to that hearing, and I talked to people there from other environmental groups. There were about twenty-five men in the room, and all of them worked for the utilities or the nuclear industry. They gave me fifteen minutes, and they had seen my paper, but I had not seen anything from them. What they had done was flown in experts from the East coast and the West coast. They had charts, and they had diagrams, and everything else. And they were given an hour to an hour and a half to expound their views. I could tell it was a rigged hearing. I was to be given a chance to speak, and they were to countermand with overwhelming amounts of information that was supposed to blow me out of the water. Towards the end I said, "I think that I should be given equal time." It

was sort of outrageous. Some of the men started looking a little sheepish; they knew what was going on.

CN: It must've been very discouraging for you.

SINCLAIR: Well, it was, because it was my first encounter with a hearing. But there were some people listening there, and this was my lesson in how the hearing process really operates. The things that you might suspect could happen, often don't, but other things do. There were two professors from the University of Michigan Nuclear Engineering Department at that meeting, and they were apparently impressed with what I said and the nature of my documentation. About a month later one of them called me and said that the University was going to put on the first Earth Day, and every department had to come up with a speaker or have some kind of a demonstration of how their particular discipline was affected by the environment. They asked me if I would present my environmental concerns. Well, that made me pretty nervous, I'll tell you, because that was going to be the toughest audience I had ever had. But I thought about it, and then I decided to go ahead and give it the best I could. So I presented it, and I had tough questions, but I felt very good about it. I felt we had a good exchange and that I had been able to hold my ground pretty well. I felt confident that I had presented them with information they might not have gotten from any other source.

Some time later I heard that one student, Richard Sandler, who had listened to me, had dropped out of his junior year in the Nuclear Engineering Department, because he decided he did not want to make a career out of a field that had so many life-threatening aspects to it. He went to Washington and became the first legislative aide on nuclear power issues. He worked for Phillip Hart, a senator from Michigan. By that time Senator Hart was getting questions on nuclear power. And so Rich Sandler handled those letters.

And some time after that I found in an obscure document the fact that all six safety tests on emergency cocoon test systems had failed. This is a very important emergency system, the ultimate backup system that the Atomic Energy Commission was depending on to prevent a meltdown, and it was their justification for putting large-sized plants near population centers. Well I knew it was very significant to the public to know that the tests had failed, but there had been nothing written about it. So I took this document along with other information I had got from a hearing that had been held on this, and I sent it to Richard Sandler. And I told him to give this information to a really good energy reporter in Washington, preferably on the *Washington Post*. He gave it to Thomas O'Toole, who is a very good energy writer on the *Post*, and O'Toole wrote an excellent story that was syndicated all over the country. After that this backup system problem appeared in every single licensing petition. The Atomic Energy Commission decided that they couldn't handle this issue in so many different places, and they decided to hold the National Safety Hearings in Washington. We were able to get sixty similar groups to join us and intervene in those hearings.

Once that National Safety Hearings started, then scientists from various laboratories on the Atomic Energy Commission, who felt that safety problems they knew about hadn't been addressed, realized that here was a national forum where these issues could be looked at. Of course, the newspapers really picked up on that, and in Washington, Congress began to be alerted to all of this. Then things began to happen. Congress passed a law that disbanded the Atomic Energy Commission because the Commission was both promoting and regulating. They established the Nuclear Regulatory Commission just to regulate nuclear power and not promote it, because Congress figured that was one of the reasons why the safety problems had not been solved. After that we got into the structure licensing hearings for Midland. One of the things that was so apparent was the quality-control breakdown they were experiencing even before the licensing started. Consumers Power had already spent $54 million on the Midland site before they even announced the public licensing hearing, and that in itself can prejudice the licensing board. When a licensing board knows that much money has been spent, they are all the more leery of finding anything wrong.

But the quality-control problems the Midland plant already had were the same kinds of things that were found previously at the Palisades plant [also in Michigan]. The Palisades plant had experienced so many quality-control problems that it hardly operated the first couple of years, and Consumers sued Bechtel, who was their builder there, and quite a few other contractors, for something like $350 million. What is strange—and I never will understand it—is how Consumers, who had this bad experience with quality-control problems with Bechtel at Palisades, turned right around and hired the same outfit to build Midland. By 1977 and '78 they discovered the full extent of the quality-control problems as far as soil compaction was concerned. That's when buildings began sinking and cracking abnormally. By August of 1978, they made their first report on the sinking and cracking of the last generator building. They reported that although the building was only twenty percent constructed, it had already sunk as much as it was expected to in forty years, and it was cracking.

Of course the NRC took great interest in that. And after a while, it became apparent that a number of other buildings were sinking and cracking. In fact, I think by November of 1978 the NRC had identified five safety-related buildings that were all affected by these problems. By December of 1979 the NRC issued an order which halted construction at the Midland plant pending their review of remedial measures to correct this soil problem. Consumers asked for a hearing on this. By asking for a hearing they were able to continue construction at Midland. And, of course, the Three Mile Island accident happened in March of 1979, and this impacted on all nuclear plants. Since the Midland plants were sister-plants to Three Mile Island, it became apparent that they had the same design deficiency.

Things were getting very intense. By this time the cost over-run and the delays were mounting terribly, but Consumers still kept insisting they were going to beat a deadline. The first time that they publicly admitted they couldn't was in April of 1983 at their annual meeting. By July of '83 Dow had cancelled their stream contract with Consumers and wanted out. Very shortly after that, Dow filed a lawsuit saying that Consumers had not disclosed to them the extent of the problems they had out there when they signed their contract. And that trial is still under way.

CN: And in July, 1984, the plant shut down.

SINCLAIR: Yes, that's right.

CN: Did you ever have any doubts throughout this fairly long process? Did you ever have any doubts about your stand? You expressed concern at one point that perhaps you had overlooked some pertinent information.

SINCLAIR: Well, that was very early, when I got this violent reaction locally. I began to say, well, I really want to be sure of my facts and study a little bit more to see if there is something I am missing; although I wouldn't have spoken out to begin with unless I had been pretty sure of my information. As a science writer and researcher, I had been trained to be very careful about these things. But I was willing to make another effort to be informed. For several years I just hoped we would be building a safer plant. But as I saw the quality control break down, not only here but elsewhere in the country, and the extent of the safety problems and how they were being dealt with or not dealt with—and also the covering-up in the industry was unbelievable—I decided nuclear power was not the way to go. I think by about the mid-1970s, I had decided it just was not right. Look at the large plants that are having serious problems and breakdowns all the time. I think that reflects the fact that nuclear power just hasn't been handled right in this country.

CN: A few hours away from Midland, the Detroit Edison Company has completed its Fermi II nuclear power plant, and that's having preliminary fuel-loading and is in the very early stages of startup. Have you had any interaction with that plant at all?

SINCLAIR: Yes, I have. I've joined the group down there in two press conferences now to try to bring issues about the Fermi plant to the public. Some of the people down there have done a pretty good job of researching the safety issues, but I was more interested in the economic issues, and these have not been publicized like they should have been. For instance, Detroit Edison today is selling more power out of the state from the excess capacity it has right now than it can expect from its share of Fermi II when the Fermi II plant goes on-line and it operates with any degree of reliability. They have so much excess capacity now that they are selling that excess capacity for about half of what they are charging their own customers.

One of their plants, the Greenwood plant, is only fully operational one percent of the time because it is oil fired and is one of the most expensive to operate. It costs six cents per kilowatt hour to operate the Greenwood plant. But when the Fermi II plant comes on line it is going to cost twenty-two cents per kilowatt hour. Twenty-two cents! And yet they are forging ahead and insisting on getting this plant on line. They don't need the power.

There have been whistle-blowers from that plant who have told about breakdowns in the computer system at Fermi II. There has been a revolution in computer technology since the Fermi plant was started in 1970, and as they have tried to update their computer design in the construction of that plant, some of the coding was not properly recorded or whatever from one system to another. These whistle-blowers claim that there is an extended period of time when you don't get the information you need from very important systems.

I think there is a separate story on the poor economics of the Fermi plant and how it's going to affect industry and business. The costs they are talking about so far don't even include the cost of waste disposal or decommissioning, which can be at least half of the construction cost of the plant. Then there's the huge volume of low-level waste these plants will generate. They don't have an answer for storing or disposing of it. I'm convinced enough that Fermi II is such an economic error that I am going to be doing what I can. It's very hard for me to do this, of course. I don't have documents all the time. I think the media should be digging into this more.

CN: What are your plans now for the future? What are you doing now?

SINCLAIR: I have been asked to give a lot of talks lately. I am going to speak in Philadelphia and in the state of Washington soon. And I've been urged to write a book. But I'd have to stop speaking in order to do the writing; they're not compatible, I find.

CN: You've been on "60 Minutes," and you've been interviewed by many major newspapers and magazines. Has that been a surprise? Has it been difficult to deal with?

SINCLAIR: It's a total surprise to me. I'm just overwhelmed. I just never expected anything like this to happen. Nor did I ever expect the Midland plant would actually shut down, to tell you the truth. I just hoped that by publicizing this they would start to do a better job. But, yes, it has been a total surprise. It was a total surprise to my family too.

CN: Do you feel like a celebrity?

SINCLAIR: I don't feel it, but people act like I am. I just feel like I'm still in the trenches, putting one foot in front of the other and trying to make something happen.

SOURCES:

PERIODICALS

Audubon, July, 1983.
Crain's Detroit Business, May 13, 1985.
Detroit Free Press, April 14, 1985.
Los Angeles Times, June 17, 1983.
Midland Daily News, December 8, 1983, July 17, 1984, May 20, 1985.
Ms., January, 1985.
Wall Street Journal, July 18, 1984.

—Sidelights and interview by Amy C. Bodwin

Peter W. Stroh

1927-

PERSONAL: Born December 18, 1927, in Detroit, Mich.; son of Gari Melchers (a brewery executive) Stroh; married 1963; wife's name, Nicole; children: two. *Education:* Princeton University, bachelor's degree, 1951; attended U.S. Brewer's Academy, 1953-54; also attended Wallerstein Brewing Seminar, 1955.

ADDRESSES: Home—Grosse Pointe Farms, Mich. *Office*—Stroh Brewery Co., 100 River Place, Detroit, Mich. 48207.

OCCUPATION: Brewery executive.

CAREER: While in school, worked summers in a boatyard and at family brewery; recruited by the Central Intelligence Agency (CIA), and worked in Washington, D.C., 1951-52, while awaiting security clearance, but a traffic accident prevented him from pursuing a career in intelligence; Stroh Brewery Co., Detroit, Mich., 1952—, member of board of directors, beginning 1965, vice-president 1965-68, director of operations, 1966-68, president, 1968-82, chief executive officer, 1980-82, chairman of board, 1982—. Member of board of directors, NBD Bancorp, Inc.; trustee, Detroit Medical Center Corp., McGregor Fund, New Detroit, Inc., and Brooks School. *Military service:* U.S. Navy, aviation training program, 1945-46.

MEMBER: United States Brewers Association (chairman, 1973-77), Economic Alliance for Michigan, Concerned Citizens for the Arts in Michigan (chairman), Economic Club of Detroit, Detroit Renaissance, Atlantic Salmon Federation.

AWARDS, HONORS: Named Humanitarian of the Year by March of Dimes, 1981; Business Statesman Award, Harvard Business School Alumni Club of Detroit, 1984.

SIDELIGHTS: With the name he carries, Peter W. Stroh bears the legacy of a 135-year-old tradition of brewing beer in Detroit, Michigan. As head of the Stroh Brewery Co., he has spearheaded the takeovers that transformed a family-owned, regional brewer into the third largest beermaker in America.

The Stroh Brewery began in 1850 with a few gallons of beer concocted in a copper kettle by Bernhard Stroh, who left Kirn, Germany, two years earlier. "He reportedly had only $150, but he invested in brewing one barrel of beer and, according to family legend, he put it on a wheelbarrow and went down the street to sell to his first customers himself," Bernhard's great-grandson Peter told Frank Angelo of the *Detroit Free Press.* From that humble beginning the company grew steadily and had the capacity—until the closing of its Detroit plant on May 31, 1985—to brew some thirty-

three million barrels, each barrel holding thirty-one gallons of beer, in seven plants across America.

In its 135-year-history, the company has withstood the challenge of fourteen years of Prohibition as well as the failures that have befallen the more than 120 American brewers that have closed in the last twenty years. In 1918, Prohibition halted Stroh Brewery's production of 300,000 barrels a year, but the company survived by branching out into soft drinks and ice cream. Stroh's continued making ice cream even after the end of Prohibition and will continue to do so in its Detroit plant. With Prohibition's repeal in 1933, the company resumed its proud fire-brewing of the traditional Bohemian Style Beer, while Peter Stroh was five years old and growing up in the elegant, monied Detroit suburb of Grosse Pointe.

Today, Stroh is considered one of Detroit's most powerful and compassionate community leaders. But he is a very private man, and he gives interviews rarely, preferring to spend his free time playing polo or hunting ducks and grouse. "He is the corporate giant who isn't listed in *Who's*

Who—a quiet, modest man who eschews awards for civic and charitable work," a *Detroit Free Press* reporter wrote.

In his own words, Stroh was "pampered" as a young man, encouraged to participate in mannered sports such as sailing, golfing and riding. He told reporter Steve Konicki of the *Detroit News*, "I think my family felt the more of those things I enjoyed doing, the more I would have in common with other people."

He went to Grosse Pointe Schools for a time and then spent several years at St. Paul's, a prep school in Concord, N.H. But Stroh's young mind was dreaming of adventure. His desire to set sail on worldwide adventure was fueled by a summertime stint at age sixteen working for a Maine sailboat owner, Jimmy Ducey. Stroh told the *Detroit News* that Ducey was scarred by polio, which had left him about "five feet tall and 80 or 90 pounds of nothing but guts and determination." "Looking back on it," Stroh continued, "of all the people I've worked for in my life, he was probably the best at what he did. He got 400 percent out of himself, so he felt that he had reason to expect 300 percent out of you."

The year after he graduated from St. Paul's, Stroh served in an aviation training program in the post-World War II Navy. The following year he spent on a waiting list trying to get into Princeton; in the meantime, he learned typing and shorthand at a Detroit business school. But he continued to dream of faraway adventure. "I wanted to unload relief supplies in Yugoslavia. I wanted to work on a tramp steamer bound for Argentina. Train polo ponies in Texas. . . seriously," Stroh told the *Detroit News*. "But I couldn't get my parents' permission."

At Princeton in 1947, he enrolled in the School of Public and International Affairs, hoping for a career with the foreign service. But the family business beckoned. The summer of 1950 saw him on the payroll of the Stroh Brewery as a plumber's helper in the maintenance department. His family figured it would give him a ground-floor view of the business. His first day of work at the brewery was the day his father, Gari Melchers Stroh, fifty-eight, then president of the company, died of lung cancer.

Upon graduation in 1951, Stroh's dream of international adventure and intrigue seemed comfortably close at hand. He was recruited by the Central Intelligence Agency (CIA), and it was with thoughts of becoming a secret agent that he worked in Washington, D.C., for a year while waiting for his security clearance. "One of my first jobs was to make photocopies of Polish agricultural journals from the war years," Stroh told the *Detroit News*. "I was described by some of my friends as becoming one of the world's ranking rutabaga experts." But just three days after he passed final security clearance, Stroh's fantasies of foreign service disappeared in the path of a runaway truck as he was crossing a Washington, D.C., intersection. The truck crushed his legs, and he was in the hospital for a year. Doctors said it was unlikely that he would ever walk again.

It was his "wonderful and wise uncle," company president John Stroh, who talked Peter Stroh out of entering the Harvard Business School after his recovery, Stroh said in November, 1984, when he received the Business Statesman

Award from the school's alumni club in Detroit. Instead of returning to the Ivy League, Stroh attended the U.S. Brewers Academy in Mt. Vernon, N.Y. in 1953-54. "It wasn't until perhaps 1954 or 1955 that I really had my legs screwed on properly," he told Konicki. "By then I had become deeply involved in the business."

By 1953, Stroh Brewery sales hit one million barrels a year for the first time and then doubled two years later. But it remained strictly a Detroit and Michigan beer. Stroh's growth began modestly in 1964, when it acquired the 91-year-old Goebel Brewing Co., which was once Michigan's leading beer producer. But by the early 1960s, the firm had fallen heavily into debt and was purchased by Stroh's for less than $2 million. In the next two years, Peter Stroh rose quickly through the corporate ranks; he was elected to the board of directors in February, 1965, became vice-president in June, 1965, and director of operations in May, 1966. He had also married his French-born wife, Nicole, in 1963. By 1968, he was the company's president, stepping into the position previously held by his uncle, John.

Through the 1970s, the appeal of Stroh's beer grew steadily in the Midwest. "From one beer lover to another. . . Stroh's" was the theme of a successful ad campaign designed to compete with the multi-million dollar media blitz of industry giants Anheuser-Busch and Miller Beer. Between 1970 and 1980, Stroh's sales more than doubled. By the end of the decade, Stroh's was among the top ten brewers in the country, a regional brewery holding its own with reported earnings of $350 million in a shrinking industry.

Hoping to expand its market beyond Michigan and neighboring states, the Stroh Brewery Company in 1981 expanded to the East Coast by acquiring the F & M Schaefer Company, the nation's twelfth-largest brewery. The purchase added Schaefer's modern Allentown, Pennsylvannia, brewery to Stroh's only existing plant, in Detroit.

Stroh's had become the nation's seventh-largest brewery and largest family-owned one when—in a takeover likened to the "minnow swallowing the whale" by some industry analysts—it bought out Milwaukee's Jos. Schlitz Brewing Company in 1982. It was one month after Peter Stroh was named chairman of the Stroh board. To buy Schlitz in 1982, Stroh borrowed more than half of the $494.7 million pricetag. It raised $170 million of that by mortgaging its Detroit brewing facilities and borrowing the money at a staggering 17.3 percent interest rate. The takeover transformed Stroh's into the nation's third-biggest brewery. From one brewery and two brands in 1978, the company went to fifteen brands and seven breweries by late 1983.

When analysts were critical of the debt the Detroit-based brewery acquired with the Schlitz purchase, Peter Stroh responded, according to a *Free Press* article, "We did not get five of the leading banks in the U.S. to lend us money in the anticipation that within two years [Stroh's] would be an entity that would not survive." But the move was also hailed because it gave Stroh's entry into the growing markets in the South and West without having to build breweries. Schlitz's plants in Winston-Salem, North Carolina, Van Nuys, California, St. Paul, Minnesota, Memphis, Tennessee, and Longview, Texas, provided the entry.

Yet the brewery's growth also came at a time when America's consumption of beer was on the downswing. Three years later, when Peter Stroh announced on February 8, 1985 that the firm's seventy-one-year-old Detroit brewery would shut down, it was because the firm found itself with too much production capacity for an American public increasingly shunning beer. In its seven breweries, Stroh's could produce more than thirty million barrels of beer, while sales in 1984 averaged about twenty-four million. By closing the Detroit plant, this margin would be erased.

"Unfortunately, our Detroit plant is our oldest and least efficient," said Stroh, according to the *Detroit Free Press*, in announcing the decision that stunned a city whose community self-esteem had been pilloried by a string of corporate pullouts. "No capital investment, concessions or any combination of these can transform it into a sufficiently viable brewery for the long term in the current industry environment. . . . I want to emphasize strongly that our need to close the plant is not a Detroit problem, a union problem, a power problem, a workers compensation problem or a utilities problem. It's just a problem of a plant that is very very old, geographically constricted and no longer competitive with the modern facilities which so dominate our industry today."

Robert Weinberg, a St. Louis-based consultant to the brewing industry, said the Stroh's decision was a good business move, although a personally agonizing one for the community-minded Peter Stroh. Said Weinberg to the *Detroit Free Press:* "To me, that is proof positive that the company is doing serious long-term planning—that the company is in the game for the long pull. They're going to do something that their senior manager must regard as personally repugnant, because it makes economic sense to do so."

But the company's fire-brewed tradition won't stop just because the block-long, red-brick Stroh complex on Detroit's near east side will be empty. Most beers are brewed with steam coils in stainless steel kettles, while Stroh's advertising boasts of a smoother flavor because it has been—and will continue to be—brewed in copper kettles over an open fire.

In addition, the Stroh Brewery and Stroh, himself, will continue a tradition of hometown civic-mindedness and community service, despite the demise of the production plant. This has been a long-standing commitment from Peter Stroh, evidenced by such efforts as the spearheading of a corporate drive to help feed the city's needy and enriching the city's riverfront. The Stroh Brewery is developing a twenty-one acre site along the Detroit River for office, retail, residential, and parking space and will maintain its headquarters at the site of this $150 million development called River Place.

Stroh was named March of Dimes Humanitarian of the Year in 1981, but it was an award he accepted reluctantly, as U.S. 6th Circuit Court of Appeals Judge Damon Keith recalled in a 1985 *Detroit Free Press* article: "I had to do a little arm-twisting to get him to accept the award. . . . He's one of the finest men I ever have met, and I can think of no one who is more committed and dedicated to the city than he is. He's so modest. He said he made a habit of not accepting any awards. He told me, 'I'm just an instrument, a little cog in the wheel.' But if you ever go to him for anything in terms of this community, any civic or charitable need, he's always willing to help."

But in Detroit—and across the nation—the name and the man will always be associated with Bohemian Style Beer. "Before we're through," Stroh told the *Wall Street Journal* in May, 1985, "we may come to the conclusion that beer is better for you than breakfast."

SOURCES:

PERIODICALS

Advertising Age, September 5, 1983.
Beverage World, October, 1983.
Business Week, December 3, 1979.
Detroit Free Press, November 4, 1975, September 14, 1983, November 21, 1984, February 9, 1985, February 10, 1985, May 3, 1985, May 10, 1985.
Detroit News, November 13, 1980, January 18, 1981, December 19, 1982.
Marketing and Media Decisions, May, 1985.
Newsweek, October 10, 1983, December 19, 1983.
New York Times, August 27, 1984.
People, December 6, 1982.
Time, April 26, 1982.
U.S.A. Today, February 24, 1983, September 6, 1983.
Wall Street Journal, May 5, 1982, June 16, 1982, September 8, 1983, February 6, 1985.

—Sidelights by Patricia Montemurri

Brandon Tartikoff

1949-

PERSONAL: Born 1949, in Freeport, Long Island, N.Y.; son of a clothing manufacturer; married Lilly Samuels (formerly a dancer with the New York City Ballet); children: Calla Lianne.

ADDRESSES: Home—Coldwater Canyon, Calif. *Office*—NBC Television Network, 3000 West Alameda Ave., Burbank, Calif. 91523.

OCCUPATION: Television network executive.

CAREER: Worked in promotion department of American Broadcasting Co. (ABC) affiliate station in New Haven, Conn., 1971-73; WLS-TV (ABC affiliate), Chicago, Ill., director of advertising and promotion, 1973-76; ABC-TV, New York, N.Y., director of dramatic programs, 1976; National Broadcasting Co. (NBC) Entertainment, Burbank, Calif., director of comedy programs, 1977-78, vice-president of programs, 1978-80, president, 1980—.

SIDELIGHTS: The youngest television executive ever to be appointed head of a network programming division, Brandon Tartikoff, president of National Broadcasting Company (NBC) Entertainment, puts NBC's ratings success—and his career—on the line every day with shows he hopes will entertain the public better than anything else in that time slot. With critical successes like "Cheers," "St. Elsewhere," and "The Cosby Show" to his credit, Tartikoff has raised NBC from its last-place ratings position, and has managed to have some fun at the same time. "I could make myself crazy worrying about how much a wrong decision will cost, so I just don't think about it," Tartikoff told the *New York Times* in 1980, shortly after being appointed to his prominent position. "My attitude is I'm going to have fun doing the job," he added, "and if it works out, fine."

Born in 1949, Tartikoff was a television baby, who claims he doesn't remember life without it. Shows like "Playhouse 90," "My Little Margie," "I Married Joan," and "Burns and Allen" filled many of his growing hours and planted ideas that would flower in the years to come. While attending Yale University, Tartikoff penned a soap opera parody that he tried unsuccessfully to persuade a local television station to broadcast. Although disappointed by the rejection, Tartikoff learned a valuable programming lesson from the director who turned him down: His own tastes should not dictate a programming choice. Tartikoff revealed the director's advice to *People* magazine: "He said, 'Take your camera to the New York bus terminal, photograph the first 100 people arriving, and whenever you make a decision think of those faces and say, "Now I like it, but will they like it?" ' "

After graduating from Yale with honors, Tartikoff landed a job in the promotion department of the same station that

AP/Wide World Photos

turned down his soap opera idea. In 1973 he transferred to the American Broadcasting Company (ABC) affiliate in Chicago, WLS-TV, where he served as director of advertising and promotion. But he longed to work in network television, and spent all his vacation time for five years in Los Angeles seeking an entree into the network elite. "It was so clear to me that I had all this talent and that anybody who had a job I wanted should step aside and invite me to help them clean out their desks," Tartikoff told *People*. "I kept setting goals and was constantly frustrated that at 23 I was still stuck in local television."

The spark that ignited Tartikoff's creative flame and gained him the recognition of high-ranking network executives came in 1976 during his stint at the Chicago station. Trying his hand at boosting station ratings, he formulated the idea of a five-day festival of ape movies called "Gorilla My Dreams Week." Impressed with Tartikoff's creativity and programming passion, WLS general manager Lew Erlicht introduced him to Fred Silverman, then ABC's programming chief. Perceiving talent, Silverman brought Tartikoff to ABC in 1976, where Tartikoff remained under Silverman's tutelage for a year as director of dramatic programs.

But Tartikoff's love of comedy lured him to NBC, where in 1977, he accepted an offer to become director of comedy programs. Within the year, Silverman also moved to NBC as president and promoted his protege to West Coast programming chief. Silverman reigned for three years as NBC's president and in 1980 named Tartikoff president of NBC Entertainment. Thus at 31 years old Tartikoff became the youngest television executive ever to be appointed head of a network programming division. Tartikoff's job revolved around the difficult task of bringing NBC out of its third-place ratings spot. When, in 1981, Silverman was replaced by Grant Tinker, Tartikoff's future seemed uncertain. Tartikoff later said that few in the industry would have been surprised if Tinker had formed his own team and dismissed Tartikoff. But Tinker did not blame Tartikoff for NBC's ratings woes. "I think he is the best guy to do the job—it's that simple," Tinker told *Time*.

Tinker's confidence in Tartikoff's hopes of creating ratings hits, however, was not enough to keep the network from losing additional viewers in Tinker's first year, with annual profits shrinking to about a quarter of those reported by first-place CBS. NBC then adopted a strategy committed to making quality the prime consideration in shows, seeking to become known as the network that would stick with new shows longer than the competition. Tartikoff supported this strategy of quality. "What an unconventional show needs is an incubation period," Tartikoff asserted in an interview with the *New York Times*. "The chance to develop an audience." Even when the early ratings of such critically-acclaimed series as the drama "St. Elsewhere," and the comedy "Cheers," both of which debuted in the fall of 1983, were disappointing, NBC stuck with them. "I don't give the public what they want," Tartikoff told *Time* "I'm more interested in giving them what they will want. I like to challenge the audience. That's not to say you don't do your share of pandering."

At least once, such so-called pandering paid off for the network. In 1983 NBC debuted "The A Team," a low-brow hit about outlaw Vietnam veterans that also earned the dubious top billing on the National Coalition on Television Violence's citing of the most violent shows on television; the series was a ratings success. But even Tartikoff acknowledged the show was not high-quality television. He claimed, however, that "The A Team" did serve a purpose by using its popular status to lead audiences into more substantive shows.

One of NBC's highest-quality shows, according to critical assessment, "St. Elsewhere" was called by *Newsweek* in 1983 the "season's most intelligent network effort as well as TV's most realistic medical series ever." Although the show initially suffered from low ratings, NBC chose to work on "St. Elsewhere" and, under Tartikoff's direction, transformed the show into one of national popularity. Tartikoff revised the scheduling and instructed writers to mix in some romance and reduce fragmented story lines to three or four per episode. Aware that "St. Elsewhere" lacked the life-and-death situation hooks that attract a viewer's attention, Tartikoff placed his convictions in the characters, telling *Newsweek* that "if the audience falls in love with the characters, the setting almost doesn't matter." He added, "This is one of the few shows I've ever taken home to run for friends before it airs."

With "Cheers," NBC's comedy series featuring regular patrons of a Boston saloon, popularity among the critics was easily won. The show premiered in a season when other network offerings were clearly inferior and was met from the outset with praise and glowing reviews from critics across the country. But critical acclaim did not initially influence the public, and "Cheers," which debuted at sixtieth out of sixty-three shows, soon fell to last place. But midway into the season, when the show was in trouble, one hopeful fact sustained its cast and crew: Tartikoff and Tinker like to watch "Cheers" because it made them laugh. Tartikoff revealed in *Esquire* that he might watch "The A Team" if he didn't have anything else to do in the hours he was home, but he was addicted to the characters of "Cheers." The series battled its way through the first season, and NBC picked it up for a second year. As Cameron Stauth of *Esquire* explained: "With all the publicity about 'Cheers' being the centerpiece of NBC's much-vaunted quality banquet of programming, Brandon Tartikoff would have had a tough time disowning this most beautiful baby of his." The show's producers relied on a combination of concern for quality, dismissal of the ratings, pressure on the press and critics to give the show free advertising, and the emergence of a cult following to turn "Cheers" into a hit. Their diligence was rewarded when "Cheers" garnered thirteen Emmy nominations.

Another of Tartikoff's ideas helped steer NBC into the number two position in the prime-time race among the three major networks by 1984: "The Cosby Show." A situation comedy created by comedian Bill Cosby about the trials of middle-aged parents, the show first aired in the fall of 1984 and proved to be a hit. It banks on the popularity of Cosby and features the kind of humor that Tartikoff has always loved. "It will remind people that all you need for a situation comedy to work and be popular is a star that they want to see and a show that is funny," Tartikoff told *Electronic Media*.

Staying one step ahead of a public demand for sensitive, though controversial, dramas has also contributed to NBC's advancement. The network's 1984 TV movie "The Burning Bed," starring Farrah Fawcett as a battered wife, even outdrew NBC's major league baseball World Series telecasts. NBC also produced "Adam," a movie about a missing child that, because of its socially provacative content, did not attract commercial sponsors. Although the viewer ratings and critical success of these movies served to reinforce what Tartikoff calls dedication to "shows we should be doing as responsible broadcasters," the reluctance of advertisers to endorse such programming may force networks to offer discounted rates. But networks cannot afford to back down from this programming, according to Tartikoff, regardless of the cost. "If we start walking away from opportunities to explore controversial subjects," he told *Electronic Media*, "those subjects are going to get explored by writers, directors and producers who will take their ideas to [cable or pay television outlets] or try to put them out as videocassettes or into theaters if need be."

As television audiences become increasingly fragmented, the networks have identified a need to diversify along with viewers by offering more than car chases, detective shows, domestic comedies and soap operas, Tartikoff asserted. But, he acknowledged, with diversification also comes the increased difficulty of convincing viewers that something innovative or unique is being shown. Even in prime time comedy, an area in which Tartikoff's career has flourished and on which NBC has built its fortune, appeal is fading. "I think the format of comedy is tired out, and so now it comes down to good writing, strong characterization and talent," Tartikoff informed *Electronic Media.*

Tartikoff points to his decision to cancel "Buffalo Bill," a short-lived serial, as one of his most difficult cancellation moves. While "Buffalo Bill" was a comedy, it differed enough from standard comedic fare that audiences were reluctant to accept it. Tartikoff explained that although the show was on the air for two different seasons, "a lot of people never even knew about it." By nature, television has discouraged producers from being adventurous with their shows, Tartikoff claimed. But NBC is committed to broadcasting comedy, even if that commitment means suffering short-term ratings setbacks. "It's just waiting for the best producers and writers to come over and do their work for NBC," Tartikoff told *Electronic Media.* "And I think that they're here because they know that we're a network that respects comedy, believes in it and is willing to sacrifice, in the short-run, the ratings and shares that we might be able to get with another type of show in order to build their shows for the long run."

In the early 1970s Tartikoff was diagnosed as having Hodgkin's disease, a cancer of the lymphatic system. At a stage in life when disease and death can seem foreign and unreal, Tartikoff was brought face-to-face with his own mortality, and with the realization that nothing in life is guaranteed. Through a regimen of chemotherapy and radiation treatments, the disease entered remission, but not without taking its toll on Tartikoff. "I used to think I was pretty hot stuff," Tartikoff told *Newsweek* when he had regained his health. "I'm still no poster child for humility, but I've got a better perspective on my priorities."

Called by *Newsweek* the "kid in TV's hot seat," Tartikoff has remained unpretentious when power and money have rewarded his achievements. With Tartikoff's prominence has also come public recognition and constant suggestions on how he should fill sixty-nine hours of programming each week. He has had ideas proposed to him in a dentist's chair, at a funeral, and in the aftermath of a car accident, while concepts have been offered by an NBC building guard as well as by U.S. President Ronald Reagan—all to feed what Tartikoff calls "the monster that never stops eating." Television, he told *People,* is that monster. "It chews things up and constantly needs replenishing," he said. Tartikoff's wife, Lilly Samuels, explained that Tartikoff does his job not for prestige but for television itself. "He loves it. At work he is so serious it's possible he frightens people. He doesn't politick, he just works," Samuels told *People* magazine. Echoed Tartikoff, "Everything I do is directed toward moving NBC into first place. It's the ideas that excite me the most."

SOURCES:

PERIODICALS

Electronic Media, September 6, 1984.
Esquire, February, 1984.
Los Angeles Times, December 22, 1982, January 13, 1984, May 23, 1984.
Newsweek, June 14, 1982, January 17, 1983, May 16, 1983.
New York Times, January 16, 1980, April 28, 1983, August 25, 1983.
People, November 12, 1984.
Playboy, June, 1982.
Time, December 3, 1984.
Washington Post, February 4, 1984.

—Sidelights by Amy C. Bodwin

Richard Thalheimer
1948(?)-

BRIEF ENTRY: Born c.1948. American marketing executive. Richard Thalheimer is founder and president of The Sharper Image, a San Francisco-based catalogue company that specializes in "toys for the executive." When Thalheimer introduced his service in the late 1970s, initial sales totaled $500,000. Today, The Sharper Image is a multi-million-dollar business catering to the whims and fantasies of young urban professionals.

Raised in Little Rock, Arkansas, in a retail-sales family, Thalheimer had always dreamed of owning a suit of armor. One item The Sharper Image offers—and its president owns—is a full-size, three-piece suit of armor that sells for close to $3,000. Thalheimer's marketing strategy is to sell articles that he himself would like to buy. His catalogue lists a variety of expensive security devices, electronic gadgets, and "fun" office furniture, including: a $250 bullet-proof vest; a $50 computerized wristwatch for joggers; a $35 light switch that is voice-activated; a $100 meter that tests the amount of salt in food; and a $900 Recaro racing car seat converted to an executive's chair.

Thalheimer credits a good deal of his success to a $129 course that he took on "How to Build a Great Fortune in Mail Order" and to the fact that direct-mail sales in general have more than doubled since 1975. Through computerized mailing lists, Thalheimer is able to pinpoint prospective customers, and he posts an average of twenty-million catalogues per year. "What you have to appreciate," he explained to Wayne King of the *New York Times*, "is that a lot of our customers are really earning big money, so it's nothing to them to spend $300 on a toy."

SOURCES:

PERIODICALS

Newsweek, November 16, 1981.
New York Times, May 1, 1982.

Terrence McCarthy/NYT Pictures

Eiji Toyoda

1913-

PERSONAL: Born September 12, 1913, in Kinjo, Nishi Kasugai, Aichi, Japan; son of Heikichi (in the family's automatic loom business) and Nao Toyoda; married Kazuko Takahashi, December 19, 1939; children: Kanshiro, Tetsuro, Shuhei, Sonoko. *Education:* University of Tokyo, B.M.E., 1936.

ADDRESSES: Office—Toyota Motor Corp., 1 Toyota-cho, Toyota-shi, Aichi 471, Japan.

OCCUPATION: Auto executive.

CAREER: Toyoda Automatic Loom Works, Aichi, Japan, trainee, 1936; Toyota Motor Co., Aichi, engineer, 1937, director, 1945, managing director, 1959-60, executive vice-president, 1960-67, president, 1967-82; Toyota Motor Corp., Aichi, chairman, 1982—. Chairman of Towa Real Estate Co. Ltd.; executive director of Toyota Central Research and Development Laboratories, Inc.; director of Aishin Seiki Co. Ltd., Toyoda Automatic Loom Works Ltd., Aichi Steel Works Ltd., and Toyoda Machine Works Ltd. Auditor, Toyoda Tsusho Kaisha Ltd.

MEMBER: Japan Automobile Manufacturers Association (president, 1972-80; supreme advisor, 1980—), Japan Motor Industrial Federation (advisor, 1980), Japan Federation Employers Association (executive director, 1967), Federation of Economic Organizations (executive director, 1967).

SIDELIGHTS: Eiji Toyoda, the man in the driver's seat of the Toyota Motor Company for nearly twenty years, is virtually unknown outside of Japan's Toyota City, headquarters of "the company that stopped Detroit," according to the *New York Times*. But like a latter-day Henry Ford, Toyoda has made his mark on the auto industry. He has not only presided over revolutionary changes in the way cars are built, he has seen his family-run business become a power-house in the world export market and has forged an unlikely alliance with an archrival, General Motors Corporation.

As chairman of one of the most powerful industrial clans in a nation of 120 million people, Toyoda has an almost Western flair as a go-getter and an empire builder that belies his reputation in Japan as a staunch political and economic conservative. The parallels between the Fords and the Toyodas extend from the assembly line to the board room. Today, the elder Toyoda shares power with his cousins: Shoichiro, who is president of Toyota Motor Corporation, and Shoichiro's younger brother Tatsuro, head of New United Motor Manufacturing Incorporated, the Toyota-GM joint venture headquartered in Fremont, Calif.

Toyoda's uncle, Sakichi, founded the original family business, Toyoda Automatic Loom Works, in 1926 in Nagoya, about 200 miles west of Tokyo. Sakichi's son, Kiichiro,

established Toyota Motor Company in 1937 as an affiliate of the loom works. The family was so involved in the business that Eiji's father Heikichi (younger brother of Sakichi) even made his home inside the spinning factory. "From childhood, machines and business were always there right in front of me," Eiji Toyoda said in an interview in *The Wheel Extended*, a quarterly review published by his company. "By seeing the two together, I probably developed an understanding of both, from a child's point of view." Toyoda describes himself as a combination engineer-administrator: "I don't really think of myself as an engineer, but rather as a manager. Or maybe a management engineer. Actually, I graduated from engineering school, but more important is the work a person accomplishes in the 10 or 15 years after school."

What Toyoda accomplished for Toyota Motor was dazzling success at a time when Detroit automakers were struggling to stay profitable. Toyota, Japan's number one automaker, spearheaded the tidal wave of small, low-priced cars that swept the United States after successive energy crises in the mid- and late-1970s. Enraged by the invasion of Japanese imports, Toyoda's counterpart at the Ford Motor Company, then-Chairman Henry Ford II, vowed, "We'll push them back to the shores." It never happened. Instead, Ford and his lieutenants turned to Toyota to negotiate a possible cooperative venture in the United States—an unsuccessful effort that preceeded GM's historic agreement in 1983 to jointly produce Toyota-designed subcompacts at an idle GM plant in Fremont.

In addition to running the largest corporation in Japan—and the world's third largest automaker, behind GM and Ford—Toyoda has overseen the development of a highly efficient manufacturing system that is being copied worldwide. It "represents a revolutionary change from certain tenets of mass production and assembly-line work originally applied by Henry Ford," wrote *New York Times* Tokyo correspondent Steve Lohr. In short, Toyoda's career could be said to echo the company's U.S. advertising slogan: "Oh, what a feeling!"

After graduating in 1936 with a mechanical engineering degree from the University of Tokyo—training ground for most of Japan's future top executives—the twenty-three-year-old Toyoda joined the family spinning business as an engineering trainee and transferred a year later to the newly formed Toyota Motor Company. The company was a relative newcomer to the auto business in Japan. The country's first car, a steam-powered vehicle, was produced just after the turn of the century, followed in 1911 by the introduction of the DAT model, forerunner of Datsun/Nissan, Toyota's nearest rival today.

The Toyoda family patriarch, Sakichi, the son of a poor carpenter, had invented the first Japanese-designed power loom in 1897 and perfected an advanced automatic loom in 1926, when he founded Toyoda Automatic Loom Works. He ultimately sold the patents for his design to an English firm for $250,000, at a time when textiles was Japan's top industry and used the money to bankroll his eldest son Kiichiro's venture into automaking in the early 1930s.

Numerous stories have sprung up over the years concerning why auto company was named Toyota rather than Toyoda. A *Business Week* article claims the family consulted a numerologist in 1937 before establishing its first auto factory: "Eight was their lucky number, he advised. Accordingly, they modified their company's name to Toyota, which required eight calligraphic strokes instead of ten. Sure enough, what is now Toyota Motor Corp. soon became not only the biggest and most successful of Japan's automakers, but also one of the most phenomenally profitable companies in the world." But a *New York Times* story notes the family changed the spelling in the 1930s because "it believed the sound [of the new name] resonated better in Japanese ears."

After Eiji joined the family business in 1936, he worked on the A1 prototype, the forerunner of the company's first production model, a six-cylinder sedan that borrowed heavily from Detroit automotive technology and resembled the radically styled Chrysler Airflow model of that period. During those early years, Toyoda gained lots of hands-on experience. "I tried in the past to see how much I could really tell by touch," he said in *The Wheel Extended*. "It was hard for me to recognize a difference of one hundredth of a millimeter. I must have had a lot of free time. Still, I think it is important to know how much of a difference one can sense." It was a philosophy he shared with his cousin

Kiichiro, who often told his employes: "How can you expect to do your job without getting your hands dirty?"

In his spare time, Eiji Toyoda studied rockets and jet engines and, on the advice of his cousin, even researched helicopters. "We gathered materials in an attempt to make a helicopter and made prototype rotary wings," he said in *The Wheel Extended*. "By attaching the wings on one end of a beam, with a car engine on the other, we built a contraption that could float in the air. . . . We weren't doing it just for fun. However, the war intensified, and it became hard to experiment because of a shortage of materials."

The war left Japan's industry in a shambles, and the automaker began rebuilding its production facilities from scratch. Recalled Toyoda: "Everything was completely new to us. Design and production, for example, all had to be started from zero. And the competitive situation allowed for not even a single mistake. We had our backs to the wall, and we knew it."

But while Kiichiro Toyoda was rebuilding the manufacturing operations, Japan's shattered economy left the company with a growing bank of unsold cars. By 1949, the firm was unable to meet its payroll, and employes began a devastating fifteen-month strike—the first and only walkout in the company's history—which pushed Toyota to the brink of bankruptcy. In 1950, the Japanese government ended the labor strife by forcing Toyota to reorganize and split its sales and manufacturing operations into separate companies, each headed by a non-family member. Kiichiro Toyoda and his executive staff resigned en masse; Kiichiro died less than two years later.

Eiji Toyoda meanwhile had been named managing director of the manufacturing arm, Toyota Motor Company. In what some automakers must view as a supreme irony, he was sent to the United States in 1950 to study the auto industry and return to Toyota with a report on American manufacturing methods. After touring Ford Motor's U.S. facilities, Toyoda turned to the task of redesigning Toyota's plants to incorporate advanced techniques and machinery. Returning from another trip to the United States in 1961, only four years after the establishment of Toyota Motor Sales USA, a prophetic Toyoda told employees in a speech recorded in a company brochure: "The United States already considers us a challenger. . . . But we must not just learn from others and copy them. That would merely result in being overwhelmed by the competition. We must produce superior automobiles, and we can do it with creativity, resourcefulness and wisdom—plus hard work. Without this . . . and the willingness to face adversity, we will crumple and fall under the new pressures."

In 1967, Toyoda was named president of Toyota Motor Company—the first family member to assume that post since Kiichiro resigned in 1950. The family power wasn't consolidated until 1981, when Sadazo Yamamoto was replaced as president of Toyota Motor Sales by Shoichiro Toyoda, son of Kiichiro and nicknamed the "Crown Prince" by the Japanese press. A year later, the two branches of the company were unified in the new Toyota Motor Corporation, with Eiji Toyoda as chairman and Shoichiro Toyoda as president and chief executive officer. A *Business Week* article at the time quoted a Japanese economist as saying the return of the Toyoda family to power was a "restoration of the bluest of blue blood."

At this stage of the company's history, there may be a strong family presence (after a stretch of non-family leadership for most of the postwar period), but not "control" in the Western sense. The top three family members own just over one percent of Toyota Motor stock, according to Britain's *Financial Times*. In contrast, the Ford family in the United States controls 40 percent of the voting power in the Ford Motor Company.

The Toyodas led their company to a record year in 1984. Toyota sold an all-time high 1.7 million vehicles in Japan and the same number overseas. Profits peaked at $2.1 billion for the fiscal year ending March 31, 1985. While that performance would certainly earn Toyota a mention in automotive history books, Eiji Toyoda and his company may be better remembered for a distinctive management style that's been copied by hundreds of Japanese companies and is gaining growing acceptance in this country. The Toyota approach, adopted at its ten Japanese factories and twenty-four plants in seventeen countries, has three main objectives: Keeping inventory to an absolute minimum through a system called *kanban*, or "just in time," insuring that each step of the assembly process is performed correctly the first time, and cutting the amount of human labor that goes into each car.

Despite the predominance of robots and automation at Toyota, the company firmly believes in the principle of lifetime employment; displaced workers are not laid off, but frequently transferred to other jobs. Toyoda believes the day when robots totally replace humans is a long way off. He told *The Wheel Extended*: "At the current stage, there is a greater difference between humans and robots than between cars and magic clouds. Robots can't even walk yet. They sit in one place and do exactly as programmed. But that's all. There is no way that robots can replace all the work of humans."

Due in part to that sort of philosophy, it's not surprising that company loyalty is so high. Toyota's 60,000 employes in Japan, for instance, are encouraged to make cost-cutting suggestions, an idea that Eiji Toyoda borrowed from Ford after his first visit to the United States. Since the system began in 1951, more than ten million suggestions have flooded the executive offices—nearly 1.7 million in 1983 alone. "The Japanese," asserts Toyoda, "excel in improving things."

SOURCES:

PERIODICALS

Automotive News, May 11, 1981.
Business Week, August 2, 1982, December 24, 1984.
Detroit Free Press, September 15, 1982, December 19, 1984, February 24, 1985, April 15, 1985.
Financial Times, August 24, 1981.
Forbes, July 6, 1981.
Fortune, July 9, 1984.
Japan Economic Journal, February 2, 1982, January 11, 1983, May 17, 1983, June 11, 1985.
Motor Trend, January, 1978.
Nation's Business, January, 1985.
New York Times, May 27, 1974, September 14, 1980, March 21, 1982, November 24, 1982.
The Wheel Extended (Toyota Motor Corp. quarterly), spring, 1984.
U.S. News and World Report, December 17, 1984.
Wall Street Journal, February 18, 1981, April 15, 1981.

—Sketch by Anita Lienert and Paul Lienert

Edward Van Halen

1957-

PERSONAL: Born January 26, 1957, in Nijmegen, Netherlands; came to United States in 1967; son of Jan (a musician) and Eugenia Van Halen; married Valerie Bertinelli (an actress), April, 1981. *Education:* Attended Pasadena City College.

ADDRESSES: Home —Hollywood Hills, Calif. *Office* —c/o Warner Brothers Records, Inc., 3300 Warner Blvd., Burbank, Calif. 91505.

OCCUPATION: Rock and roll guitarist.

CAREER: Guitarist with bands Broken Combs and Mammoth in California in the early 1970s; with band Van Halen, 1974—.

DISCOGRAPHY:

ALL WITH BAND Van HALEN; ALL PRODUCED BY WARNER BROTHERS

Van Halen (includes "You Really Got Me," "Jamie's Cryin,' " "On Fire," "Runnin' With the Devil," "I'm the One," "Ain't Talkin' 'Bout Love," "Little Dreamer," "Feel Your Love Tonight," "Atomic Punk," "Eruption," and "Ice Cream Man"), 1978.

Van Halen II (includes "Dance the Night Away," "Outta Love Again," "Somebody Get Me a Doctor," "You're No Good," "Bottoms Up!," "Women In Love. . .," "Beautiful Girls," "D.O.A.," and "Spanish Fly"), 1979.

Women and Children First (includes "Tora! Tora!," "And the Cradle Will Rock. . .," "Romeo Delight," "Fools," "In a Simple Rhyme," "Could This Be Magic?," "Loss of Control," "Take Your Whiskey Home," and "Everybody Wants Some!"), 1980.

Fair Warning (includes "Mean Street," "So This Is Love?," "Push Comes to Shove," "Sinner's Swing," "Unchained," "Dirty Movies," "Hear About It Later," "Sunday Afternoon in the Park," and "One Foot Out the Door"), 1981.

Diver Down (includes "Where Have All the Good Times Gone!," "Little Guitars," "Hang 'Em High," "Secrets," "Intruder," "Pretty Woman," "Big Bad Bill," "Dancing in the Street," "Cathedral," "Happy Trails," and "The Full Bug"), 1982.

1984 (includes "1984," "Jump," "Panama," "Top Jimmy," "Drop Dead Legs," "Hot for Teacher," "I'll Wait," "Girl Gone Bad," and "House of Pain"), 1984.

WITH OTHERS

Nicolette (with Nicolette Larson), Warner Brothers, 1978.
Thriller (with Michael Jackson), Epic, 1982.
Star Fleet Project (with Brian May and others), EMI.

SIDELIGHTS: In an era when a great deal of popular music is made by synthesized keyboards, synthesized drums, and even synthesized voices, it is the guitar that, nevertheless,

AP/Wide World Photos

remains the backbone of rock and roll. From the very beginning of the genre, it has been the raspy, raunchy wail of the electric guitar that has most eloquently characterized the rock sound.

And it is the guitar players who have invariably become the heroes of rock and roll: Scotty Moore, James Burton, John McLaughlin, Jimmy Page, Jeff Beck, Jimi Hendrix. The status of the rock guitarist was firmly established by the 1960s, when rabid fans of British guitar virtuoso Eric Clapton began scrawling "Clapton is God" in subways and on walls all over England, leaving no doubt as to who ruled the music scene.

Such hero-worship inspired countless youths to try their own hands at playing the guitar. Among them was a young Dutch immigrant, Edward Van Halen, who now ranks among the top players in the world and who, according to many accounts, may be the most inventive guitar stylist of his generation. As *Playboy* writer Charles M. Young says: "Eric Clapton used to be God. Jeff Beck and Jimmy Page were God for a while. Eddie Van Halen seems to be God right now."

Born in the Netherlands, the son of a professional clarinet and saxophone player, Van Halen was introduced to music early in life. He and his brother Alex began taking classical piano lessons at age six and continued for many years. "We had an old Russian teacher who was a very fine concert pianist; in fact, our parents wanted us to be concert pianists," Van Halen told Jas Obrecht of *Guitar Player* magazine. "I wasn't into rock in Holland at all," he explained, "because there really wasn't much of a scene going on there." But when the family moved to Southern California in 1967, "I heard Jimi Hendrix and Cream (Clapton's band at the time), and I said, 'Forget the piano, I don't want to sit down—I want to stand up and be crazy.'"

But it was Alex who was first to buy a guitar. Following his older brother's lead, Edward decided he would learn to play drums and provide accompaniment. He got a paper route and bought a drum set. Then, he told Obrecht, "while I was out doing my paper route, so I could keep up on the drum payments, Alex would play my drums. Eventually he got better than me—he could play 'Wipe Out' and I couldn't. So I said, 'You keep the drums and I'll play guitar.' From then on we have always played together."

Van Halen bought his first electric guitar, "a $70 model with four pickups," and began to copy solos—especially those of Eric Clapton—by slowing thirty-three r.p.m. records down to sixteen r.p.m. Clapton remains his biggest influence even today. In a *Rolling Stone* article, Debby Miller notes that Van Halen "asks you to name any old Cream song, and then he recreates the Eric Clapton solo, note for note. . . . Clapton is his only hero in the world,"

Miller goes on to say that "Eddie's been screwing up ever since he was a kid." He was often in trouble in school and felt that he never really fit in with the other kids. *Rolling Stone* describes him as "a geek," and Van Halen admitted to Miller that he still feels he is "much geekier" than the fans who idolize him. "Everybody," he said, "goes through teenage growing up; getting f——ed around by a chick or not fitting in with the jocks at school. I just basically locked myself up in a room for four or five years and said to myself, 'Hey, this guitar's never gonna f—— me. . . .' What I put into it, it gives me back."

While still in high school, Edward and Alex formed their first bands, Broken Combs and then Mammoth. "I used to sing and play lead [guitar] in Mammoth," Van Halen related to Obrecht, "and I couldn't stand it—I'd rather just play." They had been renting a PA system, for vocal amplification, from another Los Angeles area group, the Red Ball Jets, whose lead singer was David Lee Roth. "I figured it would be much cheaper if we just got him in the band," Van Halen says, "so he joined."

They soon added bass player Mike Anthony, who had been working in yet another local group. Anthony recalled his first encounter with Roth and the Van Halens to *Rolling Stone*'s Miller. His former band was opening for Mammoth, and "I remember standing on the side of the stage watching Edward and Alex play, and thinking, 'Wow, these guys are good.' Then Dave came up the side of the stage, and I forget what he was dressed in, some kind of a tux vest. . . with a cane and a hat. He had long hair. I don't know if he had it colored, but I know he'd done something weird to it. And he

said, 'How do you like my boys?' And I just went, 'Jesus Christ, get this guy away from me.'"

Still, Anthony was persuaded to join the group in 1974. When the subject of a new name came up, Edward and Alex voted for Rat Salade, but, according to Miller, Roth "thought it would be classier to call themselves Van Halen," and in the end he prevailed. The quartet, Edward told Obrecht, "played everywhere and anywhere, from backyard parties to places the size of your bathroom. And we did it all without a manager, agent, or record company. We used to print up flyers announcing where we were going to play and stuff them into high school lockers." They played at numerous Southern California clubs and auditoriums, performing a mixture of original material and cover tunes. Eventually they became the opening act for a number of well-known performers, including Nils Lofgren, Santana, and UFO.

During a four-month engagement at the Starwood club in Los Angeles, Van Halen came to the attention of Gene Simmons, bass player for Kiss, who financed the group's first demo tape. They were also spotted there by Marshall Berle, their future manager, who arranged for Warner Brothers vice-president Ted Templeman to come and hear them at the Starwood. "I saw their set," Templeman told Miller, "and there were like eleven people in the audience, and they were playing like they were at the Forum." Edward recalled to Obrecht that it was a "rainy Monday night in May 1977, and Berle told us that there were some people coming to see us, so play good. It ended up that we played a good set in front of an empty house." At the end of the evening, "Templeman said, 'It's great,' and within a week we were signed up. It was right out of the movies."

They began recording immediately and within three weeks had forty songs on tape. They initially picked nine of these, wrote a new one in the studio, added a couple more, and released their first LP, *Van Halen*, in 1978. Edward told *Guitar Player:* "Because we were jumping around, drinking beer, and getting crazy, I think there's a vibe on the record. A lot of bands keep hacking it out and doing so many overdubs and double-tracking that their music doesn't sound real. . . . We kept it really live." The album sold over two million copies and was followed by five others that sold well over one million copies each.

The members of Van Halen became millionaire rock stars. They were able to insist that all brown M&Ms be removed from candy bowls backstage at their concerts. And Edward, says Miller, "who used to drive to rehearsals with the doors to his car wired shut with guitar strings," bought two Lamborghinis. Their offstage antics became notorious in a business that is not easily shocked. Alex, "the band's handsomest member," according to Miller, had "the worst reputation for munching on backstage visitors." And David Lee Roth—described by *People* writer David Gritten as "a publicist's dream and a parent's nightmare"—took out insurance with Lloyd's of London against paternity suits.

But, "Eddie's idea of making an appearance at backstage parties," writes Miller, "is to dart through them slumped over, in a Groucho kind of walk, making a beeline for a closet or anywhere there's privacy." He told Gritten, "I've always been the quiet one in the band —the rest of the guys make up for me." Edward has been known to seek shelter in arena kitchens, and when Julian Lennon came to visit after a show in New Jersey, Van Halen dragged him into a bathroom for a quiet talk."

"All in all," reports Miller, "the backstage scene is calmer than it was a few years ago, when girls routinely danced nude on the tables." This is due, in part, to Mike's marriage and to Edward's well-publicized marriage to actress Valerie Bertinelli. "I don't like one-night stands," Van Halen told the *Rolling Stone* interviewer. "I don't like getting the clap. I wanna have kids. I wanna go through life with somebody."

The pairing of Van Halen and Bertinelli has puzzled many observers of the entertainment industry. She is, as Gritten puts it, "the milk-fresh sweetheart" who played the virginal Barbara Cooper on the CBS sitcom "One Day at a Time"; and he is the driving force behind a band that is often placed at the heavy-metal end of the rock and roll spectrum—not exactly the gentlest sub-category of the genre. The question on many people's minds, says Gritten, is, "What's a nice girl like that doing with a guy who plays guitar with his teeth?" The answer, replies Bertinelli, is simple: "He's not the typical rock star. It shocked *me* that he was so normal."

They met when Bertinelli's brother took her backstage at a Van Halen concert. The two entertainers were fans of each other's work, and they both admit to being very nervous. "After the concert," Bertinelli told Gritten, "we sat and talked for hours and hours. We realized we had a lot in common. We talked about our parents, Holland, how strict our upbringings had been, what it's like to be sensitive and scared of people. He has the same kind of scared feelings I have about the business." She was surprised to learn that Van Halen still lived at home with his parents. "As soon as I met them I could see why he was so normal," she recalled. "I mean, does Mick Jagger live with his mother?"

Both Catholics, Bertinelli and Van Halen go to church when they have time. They lead as quiet a life as possible in their Hollywood Hills home, and they "hardly ever go out" she says. Gritten notes that exceptions include "small dinners with friends or expeditions to watch Edward's lederhosen-clad father play sax and clarinet with a polka band in San Fernando." (The senior Van Halen has also made guest appearances on his sons' albums.)

Edward is still very close to his parents. Obrecht of *Guitar Player* asked if they ever attend Van Halen concerts, and Edward replied: "Yeah. My dad cries when he sees us play because he loves it. You know, he's so happy. It really is like his dream come true: The family music tradition is continuing, and it's also his name. . . . When I was in school, everybody said, 'Forget my parents. They're assholes.' Not me. I was always the weirdo. I'd say, 'Hey, I love my parents. I'll do anything for them. They've always busted their ass for me.' On my dad's birthday last year we retired him and bought him a boat. I want to make my people happy."

The stable family life and espousing of old-fashioned values may be atypical for a rock star, but the fact remains that Van Halen has built a reputation as the quintessential rock guitarist—wild, faster than most, and as loud as any in the

business. And he is widely recognized as one of the most influential stylists working today. As Obrecht writes, "very few guitarists have had as intense an impact in as short a time as Eddie Van Halen," who wrestles "devastating feedback, kamikaze vibrato moans, sustained harmonics, white-hot leads, and liquid screams out of a cranked-to-the-max homemade guitar."

He is often cited by rock critics and by his peers for his innovation, his creativity, and his unwillingness to rest on past accomplishments. Writes Obrecht: "In the August '79 *Guitar Player*, Ted Nugent proclaimed him 'a fantastic guitarist.' Three months later Cheap Trick's Rick Nielsen discussed Van Halen's deft use of the vibrato bar. Then in the first cover story of the '80s, Pat Travers declared Van Halen the state-of-the-art rock guitarist, adding 'I don't think there's anybody better for saying more, getting a better sound.' "

And Van Halen constantly seeks to expand the limits of his ability in order to maintain a freshness in his music. He has done flamenco-style solos on a nylon-string guitar ("Spanish Fly"), he has played with a slide on a steel-string acoustic guitar ("Could This Be Magic"), he has elicited an incredible variety of unusual sounds and noises from his homemade electric guitar, and he has perfected a unique right-hand tapping technique. The latter had become something of a trademark until a number of other guitarists began using it. Van Halen described the technique to Obrecht, saying that he hits 'a note with my left-hand finger while I tap my right index finger on the fingerboard exactly one octave up. When it's an exact octave, you bring out the harmonic plus the lower note. . . . Now this is my latest: I hammer-on and pull-off with my left hand and reach behind my left hand with my right and use my right index finger below my left hand, so that it acts as a sixth finger. In other words, my right-hand finger changes the lowest note."

Van Halen works so hard to discover new sounds, in part, because he hates to be copied. He told Obrecht: "I guess they always say that imitation is the highest form of flattery. I think this is a crock. . . . I don't like people doing things exactly like me. Some of the things I do I know no one has done. . . . What I don't like is when someone takes what I've done, and instead of innovating on what I came up with, they do my trip! They do my melody. Like I learned from Clapton, Page, Hendrix, Beck—but I don't play like them. I innovated; I learned from them and did my own thing out of it. Some of those guys out there are doing my thing, which I think is a lot different."

Van Halen's innovation carries over into live performances. He doesn't necessarily try to recreate, note-for-note, solos as he recorded them on albums, believing instead that the "feel" of rock and roll—with a measure of spontaneity—is more important than technical perfection.

In concert, Van Halen is a group that delivers everything its fans expect. Referring to a recent tour, Miller of *Rolling Stone* says, "You get a ring of fire, a phenomenal light show, loud but pristine sound and a solo in which Michael tosses his bass off a twenty-foot drop, then rolls around, wrestling it to the floor."

She calls Alex "a brilliantly musical drummer, almost as responsible as his brother for the heart-stopping power of 'Jump.'" (One time, when the band was opening for the Rolling Stones in Florida, Alex had broken his hand in four places. He tied a drumstick to his wrist with a shoelace and performed as usual.)

On stage, Roth is the focal point of the group and by far its most physical member. Miller writes: "Dave does a sword dance, jumps and kicks, and rolls over Michael's back. 'Think I could roll over Edward's back night after night? I can't even tap him on the shoulder without leaving bruises.' Dave talks to the audience, invites everyone to join him across the street for a drink."

"Whenever Eddie steps up to play a solo," continues Miller, "the kids go mad." The guitar is at the core of the group's distinctive sound, and many fans come to concerts mainly to watch Edward at work. By most accounts, they're rarely disappointed. Van Halen's philosophy, he told Obrecht, is that a rock performance must "move you in any way. Depress you, make you happy, make you horny, make you rowdy. Anything." He says that during live performances "Dave and Mike won't even come to my side because I'm so loud. But there is a difference between being just loud and having what I call a warm, brown sound—which is a rich, toney sound. I guess a lot of people are tone deaf and can't figure it out because they just crank it up with a lot of treble just for the sake of being loud. Anyone can do that. I can actually play so loud onstage that you won't hear anything else, but I don't really like to do that."

He achieves his characteristic sound with guitars that he assembles himself using primarily components made by Charvel and, more recently, Kramer. The most unusual—at least for a rock guitarist—feature of Eddie's instruments is that they usually have only one electrical pickup and only one control, a volume knob. Compared to the more common Gibson Les Paul (with two pickups, four knobs, and a switch) and Fender Stratocaster (with three pickups, three knobs, and a switch), Van Halen's guitars are stripped to the bare essentials.

He explained to Obrecht the impetus behind his desire to construct his own instruments: "A Les Paul to me was just the clichéed guitar, the rock and roll guitar. I liked the sound, but it didn't fit my body." He also wanted a guitar with a tremolo arm attachment, so he tried switching to a Stratocaster, "and Dave and Al just turned and started throwing sticks at me! They said, 'Don't use that guitar. It sounds too thin.'" It was then that he put together his own guitar with a lighter, Stratocaster-shaped body that had a sound similar to the Les Paul. Through the years, Van Halen has become quite proficient at guitar-making, and he has experimented with a great many variations and construction techniques. (One interesting technique involved removing a chunk from a guitar body with a chainsaw. It didn't work very well, he reports). But, although he now owns a fair-sized collection of instruments, including a few rare models, the guitars he uses today are basically similar to the one he put together when the group was playing high school dances.

In his personalized guitar building, in his unique playing style, and in most areas of his life, Edward Van Halen seems to have very definite ideas about what he likes and what is right for him. He doesn't care what kind of guitar other players use, and he doesn't care how other rock musicians act. "I'm not into the star bullshit at all," he told *Guitar Player*. "A lot of people get off on it—let their hair grow long, buy a Les Paul and a Marshall [amplifier], and be a rock and roll star. I don't even consider myself a rock star. I enjoy playing guitar. Period. I had an English class where I had to do an essay on what my future plans were—what I wanted to do in life. I said I wanted to be a professional rock guitarist—not a rock star."

SOURCES:

BOOKS

Guitar Player Legends of Guitar: Hendrix/Van Halen, GPI Publications, 1984.

PERIODICALS

Guitar Player, July, 1981, August, 1981, December, 1982, March, 1984, July, 1984.
New York Times, November 28, 1982.
People, November 9, 1981.
Playboy, July, 1985.
Rolling Stone, March 1, 1984, June 21, 1984.

—Sketch by Peter M. Gareffa

Andreas Vollenweider

1953-

PERSONAL: Surname is pronounced "Fole-en-veye-der"; born 1953, in Zurich, Switzerland; son of a pianist, organist, and composer.

ADDRESSES: Office—c/o CBS Records, 51 West 52nd St., New York, N.Y. 10019.

OCCUPATION: Harpist.

CAREER: Played and toured Europe for a short time with group Poetry and Music; solo performer. Composer of several film scores.

DISCOGRAPHY:

ALL RECORD ALBUMS

Behind the Gardens. . . Behind the Wall. . . Under the Tree, 1981.
Caverna Magica, CBS, 1982.
White Winds, CBS, 1985.

Also recorded three albums with group Poetry and Music.

SIDELIGHTS: He tried saxophone, and he played at the guitar, but it wasn't until Andreas Vollenweider discovered the harp that he found his musical direction. Since then, he's become one of the strongest cult acts in the music world, playing a formless combination of jazz and classical styles that is often lumped in with the improvisational "new music" approach of artists like George Winston and Keith Jarrett.

And because it's on the harp—an instrument seldom used outside of classical or baroque orchestras—Vollenweider is exploring musical territory many of his peers never imagined. "It has something to do with the way I learned the instrument," he told the *Detroit Free Press.* "I was kind of a wild animal, hard to put in school and things like that. I never had enough discipline to actually learn an instrument in school."

It seemed that Vollenweider was destined for a career in music, however. He was born in Zurich, Switzerland, in 1953, to a musical family; his father, in fact, was a prominent organist and composer. "I grew up in a family of musicians and painters and designers," Vollenweider said. "There was always creativity around me, I was never forced to do anything I didn't want to, but I'm sure that's where my interest comes from." It took a while for that interest to find a focus. His curly reddish-brown hair, lively eyes, and whimsical grin are the physical hallmarks of someone not always willing to follow prescribed rules. He described himself as a Bohemian "enfant savage" who rarely attended school and drove his music teachers crazy because he wouldn't follow the sheet music they gave him.

Instead, he learned to improvise on brass, string, and keyboard instruments, gaining proficiency through almost aimless trial and error. Then he found the harp, and it was a musical love affair. "I feel at home with this instrument," he told the *Detroit Free Press.* "I can express what I feel and my thoughts. . . . For centuries, in many different cultures, the harp had a very important place. It was more or less the bridge between spiritual things and the earthy. In the last 50 or 100 years, that's changed—it's more and more becoming the music of Walt Disney. . . . For me, the harp is incapable of a certain range of expression, the range of violence and darkness. It is an instrument of brightness and light, and therefore fits my need to counteract some of the world's negative forces. . . . The harp is [also] a very erotic instrument. I can be very erotic. When you touch it, there is no possibility of hurting it, because it sounds so perfectly beautiful when you just touch it in the first instant. It shimmers when you just touch it."

Shimmer, however, doesn't always translate into good music, and it took Vollenweider a while to pluck out the right direction for his harp-oriented creation. In the process, he played through Poetry and Music, a group that mixed mood pieces with recited poetry, recorded three albums and toured throughout Europe. Vollenweider also composed a few movie scores, but his determination not to write in dark tones to convey fear, violence and danger scared away many film producers. What he eventually settled into was "music that leaves space for the one who is listening to it, space for the creativity of the listener." It is soft, spectral, and, often, formless. Accompanied by all manners of percussion, guitar, and woodwinds, Vollenweider bends and shapes his notes by plucking the strings, lightly hammering them or caressing them up and down.

To aid his technique, he grew long fingernails, which he protects with an additional layer of false nails. He also developed a system which amplifies the harp by putting a small electronic pickup on each string. "The harp has a natural character," he explained to the *Detroit Free Press*. "To this character I've added mechanical alterations and electronics which enable me to achieve the full range of an orchestra, from the lowest notes to the highest. . . . Also, I make my own strings. The bass strings are made of silver-wound steel. They're very thick and sound very deep; I modified them electronically so they sound deeper still. Sometimes they are deeper than an electric guitar, and you can only pluck strings like that, but I wrap my thumb and middle finger with tape to protect me from the heavier gauge metal. . . . All this I've done invisibly, I hope. I don't think the sound should show how it's made. The electronics shouldn't have a life of its own."

During the early 1980s, Vollenweider was signed by CBS Records. His first two records—*Caverna Magica* and *Behind the Gardens*—sold about a million copies, mostly in Europe. In Germany, *Caverna Magica* was named 1982's best pop album by the influential *Audio* magazine, beating out Billy Joel's *An Innocent Man* and Michael Jackson's *Thriller*. America, however, wasn't deaf to Vollenweider's music. His albums became the first in history to climb *Billboard* magazine's pop, jazz, *and* classical charts. And in New York's prestigious Rizzoli bookstore, 15,000 customers bought Vollenweider records when the owners began playing it over the store's speakers.

Musicians as diverse as rock star Peter Wolf and avant-garde artist George Winston publicly admired the music. "He's just wonderful at creating textures and composing incredibly beautiful music," Winston told the *Detroit News*. "I instantly loved it." One Vollenweider fan—pop star Carly Simon—did more than pay lip service to his work. She produced his New York debut concert in October, 1984. "When I first heard Andreas' music in a store in SoHo a year ago, I knew I had discovered something that was going to change me in a wonderful way," Simon told the *New York Times*. "I became so obsessed with his music that anyone who came to my house was introduced to it within the first 10 or 15 minutes."

CBS started to realize what it had when statements like that began to appear in print. For Vollenweider's first American tour in late 1984, the company hired a high-powered California publicity firm that usually handles rock acts to pump the press. And in early 1985, CBC prepared a full-scale campaign for his new album, *White Winds*.

The efforts helped sell more records, though it's unlikely Vollenweider will ever reach the sales ranks of Jackson or Joel. Not that it matters to him; he's happy with a marginal degree of popularity and surprised at the size of his following. "I am, of course, excited," he said in a *Detroit Free Press* interview. "I didn't expect it all, what happened [in America]. It's getting to be like it was in Europe—and I didn't expect what happened there, either."

SOURCES:

PERIODICALS

Detroit Free Press, October 24, 1984.
Detroit News, May 23, 1985.
Newsweek, May 13, 1985.
New York Times, October 19, 1984.
Wall Street Journal, October 24, 1984.

—Sidelights by Gary Graff

Peter C. Wilson

1913-1984

AP/Wide World Photos

OBITUARY NOTICE: Born March 8, 1913, in Yorkshire, England; died June 3, 1984, in Paris, France. Art auctioneer and business executive. As chairman of Sotheby & Co. from 1958 until his retirement in 1980, Peter C. Wilson transformed the auction house from a small, centuries-old fine arts concern to an international, $575-million-per-year firm that widely influences the world art market. Educated at Eton and Oxford University, Wilson once considered a career in journalism. He briefly worked for the Reuters news agency and for *Connoiseur,* an art magazine. He joined Sotheby's in 1936 and two years later became a partner and director. During World War II Wilson served with British Intelligence in London and New York, returning to Sotheby's shortly after the war.

Wilson's first successful attempt to expand his company's operations took place in 1954, when he arranged the sale of deposed King Farouk's art collection. Four years later Wilson was named Sotheby's chairman. Within weeks of his appointment he had acquired a collection of Impressionist and Post-Impressionist paintings from the estate of New York financier Jakob Goldschmidt. The collection, which included works by Cezanne, Van Gogh, and Renoir, sold for an unprecedented $2,186,800. The Goldschmidt sale ushered in the era of multimillion-dollar art auctions and firmly established Wilson's name in the art world.

In 1964 Wilson engineered the purchase of New York's Parke-Bernet & Co., the largest art auction house in the United States. Under his direction Sotheby's opened offices and galleries in thirty-six cities around the world. Due to Wilson's vast knowledge of art and shrewd commercial instinct, Sotheby's enjoys a reputation as a thriving, innovative enterprise. It became the first auction establishment to open sale outlets outside its own country and the first to employ computers and closed-circuit and satellite television. Wilson was made Commander, Order of the British Empire in 1970.

SOURCES:

BOOKS

Current Biography, Wilson, 1968.

PERIODICALS

London Times, June 5, 1985.
New York Times, November 10, 1979, August 30, 1980.

Cumulative Newsmaker Index

Cumulative Nationality Index

AMERICAN
Allred, Gloria **1985**:2
Alter, Hobie
Brief Entry **1985**:1
Anastas, Robert
Brief Entry **1985**:2
Arquette, Rosanna **1985**:2
Basie, Count
Obituary **1985**:1
Beattie, Owen
Brief Entry **1985**:2
Bell, Ricky
Obituary **1985**:1
Boone, Mary **1985**:1
Boyer, Herbert Wayne **1985**:1
Brown, Willie L. **1985**:2
Bushnell, Nolan **1985**:1
Clements, George **1985**:1
Colasanto, Nicholas
Obituary **1985**:2
Coors, William K.
Brief Entry **1985**:1
Cox, Richard Joseph
Brief Entry **1985**:1
De Cordova, Frederick **1985**:2
Diamond, Selma
Obituary **1985**:2
Dolan, Terry **1985**:2
Donghia, Angelo R.
Obituary **1985**:2
Engstrom, Elmer W.
Obituary **1985**:2
Ervin, Sam
Obituary **1985**:2
Falkenberg, Nanette **1985**:2
Ferrell, Trevor
Brief Entry **1985**:2
Gibson, Kirk **1985**:2
Gooden, Dwight **1985**:2
Gould, Chester
Obituary **1985**:2
Grant, Charity
Brief Entry **1985**:2
Hagler, Marvelous Marvin **1985**:2
Hancock, Herbie **1985**:1
Harris, Patricia Roberts
Obituary **1985**:2
Hefner, Christie **1985**:1
Hernandez, Willie **1985**:1
Horner, Jack **1985**:2
Hullinger, Charlotte
Brief Entry **1985**:1

Inman, Bobby Ray **1985**:1
Jarvik, Robert K. **1985**:1
Kloss, Henry E.
Brief Entry **1985**:2
Knight, Philip H. **1985**:1
Kroc, Ray
Obituary **1985**:1
LaFontaine, Pat **1985**:1
Lauper, Cyndi **1985**:1
Lightner, Candy **1985**:1
Lipsig, Harry H. **1985**:1
Lithgow, John **1985**:2
Lodge, Henry Cabot
Obituary **1985**:1
Long, Shelley **1985**:1
Madonna **1985**:2
McGowan, William **1985**:2
Monaghan, Tom **1985**:1
Musburger, Brent **1985**:1
Olajuwon, Akeem **1985**:1
Ormandy, Eugene
Obituary **1985**:2
Petersen, Donald Eugene **1985**:1
Pittman, Robert W. **1985**:1
Potok, Anna Maximilian
Brief Entry **1985**:2
Quinlan, Karen Ann
Obituary **1985**:2
Retton, Mary Lou **1985**:2
Roche, Kevin **1985**:1
Rock, John
Obituary **1985**:1
Schlessinger, David
Brief Entry **1985**:1
Sinclair, Mary **1985**:2
Stroh, Peter W. **1985**:2
Tartikoff, Brandon **1985**:2
Thalheimer, Richard
Brief Entry **1985**:2
Van Halen, Edward **1985**:2
Wells, Sharlene
Brief Entry **1985**:1
Wigler, Michael
Brief Entry **1985**:1
Woodruff, Robert Winship
Obituary **1985**:1

BRITISH
Wilson, Peter C.
Obituary **1985**:2

CANADIAN
Garneau, Marc **1985**:1
Haney, Chris
Brief Entry **1985**:1
Lalonde, Marc **1985**:1
Pocklington, Peter H. **1985**:2

FRENCH
Chagall, Marc
Obituary **1985**:2

GERMAN
Mengele, Josef
Obituary **1985**:2

INDIAN
Gandhi, Indira
Obituary **1985**:1

ISRAELI
Arens, Moshe **1985**:1

JAPANESE
Miyake, Issey **1985**:2
Toyoda, Eiji **1985**:2

LEBANESE
Berri, Nabih **1985**:2

NICARAGUAN
Cruz, Arturo **1985**:1

NIGERIAN
Olajuwon, Akeem **1985**:1

SPANISH
Miro, Joan
Obituary **1985**:1

SOVIET
Chernenko, Konstantin
Obituary **1985**:1
Gorbachev, Mikhail **1985**:2
Brief Entry **1985**:1

SWISS
Vollenweider, Andreas **1985**:2

Cumulative Occupation Index

This index lists all newsmakers by their occupations or fields of primary activity.

ART AND DESIGN
Boone, Mary **1985**:1
Chagall, Marc
    Obituary **1985**:2
Donghia, Angelo R.
    Obituary **1985**:2
Miro, Joan
    Obituary **1985**:1
Miyake, Issey **1985**:2
Potok, Anna Maximilian
    Brief Entry **1985**:2
Roche, Kevin **1985**:1
Wilson, Peter C.
    Obituary **1985**:2

BUSINESS
Alter, Hobie
    Brief Entry **1985**:1
Boyer, Herbert Wayne **1985**:1
Bushnell, Nolan **1985**:1
Coors, William K.
    Brief Entry **1985**:1
Cox, Richard Joseph
    Brief Entry **1985**:1
Engstrom, Elmer W.
    Obituary **1985**:2
Haney, Chris
    Brief Entry **1985**:1
Hefner, Christie **1985**:1
Kloss, Henry E.
    Brief Entry **1985**:2
Knight, Philip H. **1985**:1
Kroc, Ray
    Obituary **1985**:1
McGowan, William **1985**:2
Monaghan, Tom **1985**:1
Petersen, Donald Eugene **1985**:1
Pittman, Robert W. **1985**:1
Pocklington, Peter H. **1985**:2
Schlessinger, David
    Brief Entry **1985**:1
Stroh, Peter W. **1985**:2
Tartikoff, Brandon **1985**:2
Thalheimer, Richard
    Brief Entry **1985**:2
Toyoda, Eiji **1985**:2
Wilson, Peter C.
    Obituary **1985**:2
Woodruff, Robert Winship
    Obituary **1985**:1

EDUCATION
Clements, George **1985**:1

ENTERTAINMENT
Arquette, Rosanna **1985**:2
Basie, Count
    Obituary **1985**:1
Bushnell, Nolan **1985**:1
Colasanto, Nicholas
    Obituary **1985**:2
Cox, Richard Joseph
    Brief Entry **1985**:1
De Cordova, Frederick **1985**:2
Diamond, Selma
    Obituary **1985**:2
Gould, Chester
    Obituary **1985**:2
Hancock, Herbie **1985**:1
Haney, Chris
    Brief Entry **1985**:1
Hefner, Christie **1985**:1
Lauper, Cyndi **1985**:1
Lithgow, John **1985**:2
Long, Shelley **1985**:1
Madonna **1985**:2
Musburger, Brent **1985**:1
Ormandy, Eugene
    Obituary **1985**:2
Pittman, Robert W. **1985**:1
Tartikoff, Brandon **1985**:2
Van Halen, Edward **1985**:2
Vollenweider, Andreas **1985**:2
Wells, Sharlene
    Brief Entry **1985**:1

LAW
Allred, Gloria **1985**:2
Brown, Willie L. **1985**:2
Ervin, Sam
    Obituary **1985**:2
Lightner, Candy **1985**:1
Lipsig, Harry H. **1985**:1

**POLITICS AND
GOVERNMENT—FOREIGN**
Arens, Moshe **1985**:1
Berri, Nabih **1985**:2
Chernenko, Konstantin
    Obituary **1985**:1
Cruz, Arturo **1985**:1
Gandhi, Indira
    Obituary **1985**:1
Garneau, Marc **1985**:1
Gorbachev, Mikhail **1985**:2
    Brief Entry **1985**:1
Lalonde, Marc **1985**:1

**POLITICS AND
GOVERNMENT—U.S.**
Brown, Willie L. **1985**:2
Dolan, Terry **1985**:2
Ervin, Sam
    Obituary **1985**:2
Falkenberg, Nanette **1985**:2
Harris, Patricia Roberts
    Obituary **1985**:2
Inman, Bobby Ray **1985**:1
Lodge, Henry Cabot
    Obituary **1985**:1

RELIGION
Berri, Nabih **1985**:2
Clements, George **1985**:1

SCIENCE
Beattie, Owen
    Brief Entry **1985**:2
Boyer, Herbert Wayne **1985**:1
Garneau, Marc **1985**:1
Horner, Jack **1985**:2
Jarvik, Robert K. **1985**:1
Rock, John
    Obituary **1985**:1
Wigler, Michael
    Brief Entry **1985**:1

SOCIAL ISSUES
Allred, Gloria **1985**:2
Anastas, Robert
    Brief Entry **1985**:2
Clements, George **1985**:1
Coors, William K.
    Brief Entry **1985**:1
Falkenberg, Nanette **1985**:2
Ferrell, Trevor
    Brief Entry **1985**:2
Grant, Charity
    Brief Entry **1985**:2
Hefner, Christie **1985**:1
Hullinger, Charlotte
    Brief Entry **1985**:1
Lightner, Candy **1985**:1
Lodge, Henry Cabot
    Obituary **1985**:1
Mengele, Josef
    Obituary **1985**:2
Quinlan, Karen Ann
    Obituary **1985**:2
Sinclair, Mary **1985**:2

Cumulative Subject Index

This index lists key subjects, company names, products, organizations, issues, awards, and professional specialties.

Cumulative Subject Index